Pause and Reverse

Pause and Reverse

HOW TO LOOK YOUNGER THAN YOUR AGE WITH OR WITHOUT COSMETIC SURGERY

Brett Kotlus, M.D.

ISBN: 0692421785
ISBN 13: 9780692421789
Library of Congress Control Number: 2015905406
Austin Street Publishing, long island city, NY

For Ruth, my centenarian grandmother, who epitomizes beauty and longevity.

Contents

Preface

A World without Wrinkles?

As it stands, a world without wrinkles cannot exist. Your skin, muscles, organs, and skeleton are part of a wondrous machine that was perfectly designed to be imperfect. Wrinkles and aging are coded in your DNA, the essential blueprints for your body. You can modify how these blueprints are translated into your person by altering your environment, your food intake, and your lifestyle, but some of the visible perils of aging are unavoidable, at least until designer humans can be made with targeted gene therapy, nanomachines, and 3D-printed organs. I talk about these tools at length in the "Cosmetic Treatments of the Future" chapter.

My original title for this book, *A World without Wrinkles*, evoked images of a *Twilight Zone* episode or *The Stepford Wives*. What if expressions were blunted or absent because we couldn't smile or raise our brows? Imagine how creepy it would be to walk down a crowded street surrounded by shiny porcelain faces and not know which of your neighbors was the grandparent, the parent, or the teenager.

So, I changed the title to *Pause and Reverse* because it describes the strategy I recommend to my patients on a daily basis, and it's clearly preferable to look youthful and normal rather than flawless and plastic.

A fantasy world without wrinkles does exist in fashion media and celebrity portraits. Digital image manipulation with Photoshop and other programs has become standard practice in the industry, and blemishes and wrinkles are seldom seen. There has been some backlash against these practices, but they remain prevalent for the most part. HD television broadcasts show us a glimpse of the humanity of our newscasters who can no longer obscure their facial details behind the poor-quality optics of tube televisions. However, at the checkout stands at the supermarkets, we are still fed images of actors who appear ageless and unchanged over decades in the public eye. In a way, we want to believe that these people are ageless. Perhaps it distracts us from the fact that we ourselves are aging. However, when one of these celebrities undergoes a cosmetic procedure that looks slightly (or blatantly) unnatural, the celebrity is demonized. The ideal in our society is an ageless but appropriate look. Many people compare themselves to an unattainable media aesthetic, and they are left confused and insecure about their self-image.

Some people want to live in an unwrinkled world. I urge you to avoid this trap. Your twenties may have been your last truly wrinkle-free years or maybe your thirties if you are lucky to have the right combination of genes. However, you can't look like a twentysomething for the rest of your life. If you accept this now, you will save yourself some unneeded stress. I'm not advocating that you surrender to the aging process, but you do need to accept that you are subject to its effects. Seventy-year-olds who are desperately clutching to their visions of themselves as twenty-two-year-olds by way of cosmetic treatments and surgery do not look natural and certainly do not look good. Seventy-year-olds who look fifty-five because they took great care of their skin and had a few selective enhancements done look younger than their friends, leaving everyone wondering how they managed to beat the evil forces of time.

Even if a world without wrinkles could exist, it probably wouldn't. It would require a global movement in which the entire human population subscribed to the same aesthetic ideals, and every person would simultaneously need the resources to act upon these ideals. The world has more pressing issues— like despotism and political conflict, nuclear threats, global warming, and starvation, to name a few.

We agree that a world without wrinkles is not a global priority. Let us also agree, then, that a world with fewer wrinkles is a worthy personal goal for many of us. In a world with fewer wrinkles, we are all more diligent about skin health and restorative measures that help us maintain our youthfulness inside and out. We feel good about our looks and ourselves, but we don't look phony or need to be Photoshopped.

Introduction

Let's be honest. You don't *need* any cosmetic treatments. With few exceptions, they are luxuries, but absolutely nothing is wrong with wanting them. In fact, in well-selected situations, cosmetic procedures are positive, confidence-boosting tools. You've lived in your body for a while now, and you care about how it looks. You probably brush your hair in the morning. You wear clean clothing that complements your body's frame, and you tend to choose styles that say something about your fashion sense. You may adorn yourself with a watch or earrings or a necklace that just looks nice. You do these things because you care about how you present yourself to others. You're not alone if you feel some hesitation at the idea of "having something done." Many of my patients have expressed that they feel guilty or anxious when considering doing something cosmetic. Ultimately, you will decide what you do for yourself, and it is OK to do something for yourself—not that you need my permission. I hope that you are proud of who you are and how you look, and that doesn't make you vain.

The word *vanity* carries a negative connotation—that you care *too much* about how you look. Your attitude about your appearance falls somewhere on a spectrum, and it can only be evaluated within the context of your specific cultural setting. Different cultures and social groups have differing parameters that dictate what is acceptable in terms of beauty, appearance, and cosmetic practices. Cosmetic rituals and body modification have been part of many cultures throughout history, and they have been widely accepted as a form of expression and ornamentation. Arabic texts that date back to approximately AD 1000 describe the treatment of hanging upper-eyelid skin with cauterization (a controlled burn) to shrink the skin. In the Renaissance era, scores of European women plucked the hairs at the tops of their foreheads because a high hairline was considered a sign of beauty and elevated social status. Today, some African tribes maintain the ancient custom of adorning themselves with large, disk-shaped lip plates as a marker of social and economic position. These practices, which may seem drastic or un-appealing, are or were not only accepted but also embraced within their given communities, just as a hair perm or an eyebrow wax may seem odd to an individual from a vantage point different from ours.

Our own culture can be divisive regarding cosmetic practices. On one side, a person wants to fight the signs of aging tooth and nail. He or she will accept and seek out treatments, procedures, injections, and surgeries that will help to maintain youthfulness and, in some cases, change facial features to match a perceived image of youth. Such people tend to feel youthful in spirit and want to manifest externally that feeling. I believe there is also an aspect of nostalgia that feeds this desire. If someone considers youth the best years of life, that person naturally wants to hold on to the feelings and experiences from that time and may strongly identify with the youthful version of him- or herself. I think the innate desire for longevity is often accompanied by a desire to extend the young-feeling (and young-looking) years into middle and later life. On the other hand, a person may or may not be concerned with looks but does not want to make any modifications or treatments whatsoever. Regardless of whether this person acts or feels young, he or she believes that the external signs of aging should be allowed to proceed without any interference. Most of us fall somewhere in between these two viewpoints.

My purpose is not to convince you to go out and have cosmetic surgery. The aims of this book are to help you maintain your face's natural beauty, to pinpoint the source of any concerns you may already have about your appearance, and to inform and guide you in regard to effective solutions for your concerns. Some solutions are surgical, but many are nonsurgical. I want to help you sort through the myriad of confusing and sometimes flashy remedies offered by the cosmetic industry.

Who Am I to Offer Advice?

My perspective is that of a medical doctor. After college I earned a graduate degree in genetics, work-ing with special strains of laboratory mice for two years and helping to discover some of the genes responsible for tasting behaviors (such as sweet, sour, and bitter). After my rodent-intensive research, I decided I wanted to spend more time with people. My strength in the sciences led me to attend medical school. I continued my medical training with a yearlong internship in internal medicine in Denver, Colorado. I completed a residency in ophthalmic surgery (microsurgery of the eyes and surrounding face) in New York. I then completed two postresidency fellowships in cosmetic surgery and ophthalmic plastic surgery in Arizona. After this lengthy specialty training (I have plenty of gray hair to attest to its duration), I began to practice functional oculofacial surgery (plastic surgery of the eyelids and face) and cosmetic surgery. For eight years, I was the primary cosmetic surgeon in one of the country's largest aesthetic medical practices, in Michigan. Then I relocated back to New York City, where I was born, to start my own cosmetic practice. A major part of my career is being a continual student, and I continue to learn about new products, devices, lasers, and surgical procedures. I want to share my extensive experience and informed opinions with you.

When I told some of my colleagues that I was writing a book about facial aging and cosmetic treatments, the overwhelming advice I received was "don't do it." This surprised me, but I understood their perspective. They said that I would lose potential patients if I gave away all of my expertise and that I should hold on to this information because it adds value to my consultations. I disagreed. Everything in this book is already out there in medical journals and on the Internet. I have simply distilled the points that I think are valuable, relevant, and true.

Don't Put This Book Down without Reading the Next Two Points

In our culture, two cosmetic facial concerns deserve your attention no matter what. The rest are optional but may be appropriate, based on your personal beauty or health goals.

1. You need to wear sunscreen to reduce your risk of skin cancer, and you need to monitor your skin for suspicious growths. These are irregularly shaped spots that may have grown larger or have nonuniform color. I've had a good deal of experience with the devastating effects of skin cancer as a surgeon at the VA hospital in sunny Tucson, Arizona. There was a saying that every patient had a spot of skin cancer if you looked hard enough. I performed an extraordinary number of reconstructive facial procedures on these patients after skin cancer removal. Many cancers could have been avoided if the merits of facial sunscreen had been emphasized fifty years ago. My own wife has dealt with facial skin cancer, and it has made me even more vigilant about sun protection.

2. You also need to be aware if your upper-eyelid skin is sagging so much that it is getting in the way of your vision. This sounds strange, but as we age, our upper lids tend to stretch and sag. When they stretch enough, they obstruct your peripheral view when driving and doing other daily tasks. As you can imagine, excess eyelid skin can be dangerous and lead to injury.

Start by Looking Inward

At the beginning of an antiaging, beauty-preserving, or feature-refining treatment plan, you should engage in self-reflection. What is your motivation? I hope that you ultimately conclude that your decision comes from a healthy place and your family and loved ones support you in your decision. This may not be as important regarding a new skin-care regimen, but it's definitely beneficial to have support when you are recovering from a major or even a minor surgery.

Don't change something about your looks to impress someone or to get back at an ex. Don't have a surgery because you think it will be the one link to a perfect life. Don't expect that you are going to win someone's love with a laser or a plumping injection. Don't try to look like a celebrity because he or she is the Hollywood flavor of the week. Do it for you. Do it because you like the way you look, and you want to extend that beauty for many years. Do it to refine and preserve your own special features. Do it to put forth a youthful, vivacious version of you to the world.

Where to Have Work Done

When you seek a cosmetic product or procedure, you will have to choose a source or a provider. This is a personal and important decision. For over-the-counter skin-care products, it's acceptable to use multiple sources of information. Aestheticians, beauty magazines, television health programs, and physician blogs can help guide you. For medical-grade cosmeceuticals and prescription medications, you need to see a physician, physician's assistant, or nurse practitioner. It should go without saying that surgery and laser treatments should only be sought from experienced doctors in properly equipped facilities. Definitely avoid hotel-room injections. (You may have read some horror stories in the news about industrial silicone injections being performed in questionable settings.)

There is overlap among medical specialties that provide cosmetic services. Don't buy into the hype that you must only see a certain type of doctor for everything cosmetic. This myth is fed by the political and financial motivations of specific interests. Truthfully, you can receive expert Botox and filler injections from a variety of specialists. These might include a dermatologist, oculoplastic surgeon, otolaryngologist, plastic surgeon, or nurse in select cases. The skill of the injector is based on training and experience. For surgical procedures, again, you want to rely on training and experience. These key elements are not always reflected in the placard your provider displays on the wall. For example, a good many board-certified plastic surgeons do not have extensive cosmetic training, and some cosmetically oriented ear, nose, and throat surgeons are masterful at aesthetic eyelid surgery.

When you interview prospective medical providers, ask how many procedures they have done. Ask for referrals, and ask to see examples of their work. (However, be aware that they will show you only their best results, not their worst.) Ask about their cosmetic training. Did they do a cosmetic fellowship or did they have comprehensive cosmetic training in their residency? With regard to some of the newer lasers and injectables, it is not possible that someone who completed his or her residency ten years ago had direct training in these exact procedures. He or she will have acquired these skills after formal residency. That is the nature of the aesthetic field. There will always be new technologies, and at first, there may not be a doctor who has more than twenty treatments under his or her belt. In those situations, you may want to wait at least six months to a year to see how a new procedure fares with others. You may want to ask friends or family members if they have provider recommendations. However, the right doctor for someone else might not be the right one for you. You should feel that you have chosen a doctor who makes you feel comfortable, who listens to your goals as you express them, whose credentials and experience are acceptable to you, and who has an aesthetic sense that matches yours.

You must have a sense of trust to be able to place yourself in someone's hands. Is the salesperson at the department-store sales counter giving you unadulterated advice, or is he or she working to enhance his or her sales quota? You will encounter providers who mainly push their newest product or laser. Is it the best, most advanced technology that only recently became available or are they trying to keep up with their monthly installments on the expensive device? It could be a combination of both. Your provider may have a conflict of interest when making a suggestion about your beauty. That is not to say that you should expect everyone in the field to try to take advantage of you. You just need to do some research on new products or devices and feel that your provider is trustworthy. Again, recommendations from someone close to you can go a long way.

There are plenty of online resources to help you investigate a procedure or a provider. These include doctor rating sites, RealSelf.com, your state's medical board or professional health-licensing site, and many more. You'll have to take the anonymous review sites with a grain of salt because they can be filled with fake or unfairly solicited ratings and comments from the providers or manufacturers themselves (in the case of overwhelmingly positive reviews) or from competitor providers or disgruntled former employees (in the case of horrifically scathing reviews).

Do No Harm

A doctor who provides cosmetic services is in an unusual situation. Part of an oath often taken upon medical-school graduation (not all graduates take this oath) includes a statement that as a physician, one should do no harm. In a sense, cosmetic surgery does cause harm. A cosmetic nose surgery, for example, involves incisions on the nose skin and possible removal of cartilage and bone that could certainly have been left alone, thereby avoiding some health risks associated with surgery and anesthesia. Cosmetic surgery, in order to achieve a certain endpoint, leaves behind controlled injuries. The rationale for intentionally causing some harm is that the overall outcome will be beneficial for the patient's well-being, and after the physical injuries have healed, the patient is in a more content psychological place. You and your cosmetic provider will have to weigh the possible risks with the potential benefit of any procedure before you proceed.

The rewards of a well-selected and well-executed cosmetic procedure or a properly tailored skin-care regimen can be profoundly gratifying. I see this every day with my many happy patients and clients. I even see it for myself in the mirror as the result of my own simple skin-care regimen of several years. I sincerely hope that you will see the same results for yourself as you read this book and take the next steps to achieve your most youthful-looking self.

CHAPTER 1

The Science of Looking Older

You may have experienced the harrowing moment when you look in the mirror and asked why. Why is my face sagging? Why am I seeing more wrinkles? Why am I looking progressively more like one of my parents? We all know deep down that we look older because we are older. It's a natural instinct to ask why because somehow understanding the mechanisms of aging can provide insight into how to avoid and reverse some of the visible signs of aging.

Medically speaking, aging can be observed on a molecular level, a cellular level, and an organ level. After the early developmental years, aging is generally seen as a continuous process of deterioration. Some aging processes are preprogrammed, meaning they are coded in your DNA. Menopause, collagen and elastin degradation, graying hair, and bone loss are all tightly linked to internally coded aging. Others may be a result of our environment, the so-called "wear and tear" aging. These environmental aging processes include gradual joint deterioration, sun damage, effects of chemicals and pollutants, and the effects of the continuous force of gravity on your body.

The Molecular Aging Theories

The Free-Radical Theory

Free radicals are unstable molecules. They tend to be unstable because they have unpaired electrons, the negatively charged subatomic particles. These free radicals cause damage to important DNA and proteins in our bodies by stealing electrons and potentially altering their structure and function. Radiation, for example, can create damage-causing free radicals. This damage is called oxidation, and it injures our cells and can initiate mutations in the genetic coding found in our cells. Some believe that we age due to the cumulative effects of free radicals. However, we have enzymes in our bodies that are antioxidants, meaning they prevent oxidative damage from free radicals by replacing missing electrons. Antioxidants can also be found in our diets (e.g., vitamin C). We can theoretically slow down our aging processes with antioxidants. This is why we hear so much about them in skin products, food labeling, and supplements. The free-radical theory does hold credibility, but other aging processes take place at the same time that should be considered.

The Telomere Theory

The telomere theory of aging is based on the observation that as our cells divide and replenish, the end pieces of our DNA shorten. With each cell division, these DNA caps called telomeres lose some length, and the length of the cap provides information about how many divisions remain in that cell. In a sense, the telomere is an aging clock built into our genetic code. Once the telomere is gone, further cell divisions will shorten the important DNA for protein coding, and the cell will become nonfunctional. It's possible that this process can be halted by preventing the degradation of telomeres with protective molecules or with an enzyme called telomerase that replaces lost telomeres. This theory is often debated, and there is not much that we can currently do ourselves to alter this process.

The Mitochondrial Theory

Another theory postulates that mitochondria, the structures that provide energy to your cells, gradually lose their efficiency and are unable to power your cells over time. These power-producing cell subunits are found in all of your cells, and they have their own genetic code that is separate from other DNA in your body. The mitochondrial DNA is more susceptible to oxidative damage and free radicals than your other DNA. When the mitochondria slow down, the other parts of the cell that are necessary for essential functions, such as protein production, become less functional. Coenzyme Q (CoQ_{10}) helps to protect against free-radical damage to the mitochondria, and it has been shown that the older we are, the less CoQ_{10} we have in our tissues. However, most studies have not shown significant antiaging benefits from CoQ_{10} dietary supplements.

2

Aging of Your Organs

Your skin, the body's largest organ by surface area, exhibits several forms of degradation with age. The outermost layer of skin, the epidermis, becomes thinner. This causes more noticeable creases when making facial expressions as well as more fixed or static lines even without expressions. Collagen and elastin proteins (responsible for the stretchiness or elasticity of skin) become less numerous in your skin, leading to less suppleness and recoil. This explains why the skin on the back of a child's hand snaps back instantly when pinched. When you pinch the back of an eighty-year-old's hand, the skin takes longer to snap back. It tends to linger, as if saying, "Give me some time; I'm tired."

With age, pigment cells (melanocytes) within the skin show increased production of melanin, resulting in more brown spots, also known as liver spots or age spots.

Significant bone mass is gradually lost after the age of forty. By the age of eighty, you may have lost a few inches of your overall height. Loss of facial bone mass means less support for the overlying muscle, fat, and skin, producing an increasingly gaunt, sunken, and aged appearance.

Facial fat tends to atrophy or shrink with age while the fat around the eyeball (that has a different embryologic origin) tends to increase in size. This means the cheeks, temples, and jawline all appear to deflate and sag while the areas under the eyes demonstrate fat bulges or bags. Connective tissue between the layers in the face also degrades, leading to a loss of support and firmness. When it seems that gravity is pulling down on our facial skin and causing it to sag, our faces are actually deflating and losing connective tissue support, like a smooth grape gradually drying to become a shrunken, wrinkled raisin.

Some of the connective tissue structures in our faces are sturdier than other structures. When a tight, well-supported area on your face lies below a looser area, the skin will fold. This occurs at the nasolabial creases, the lines running from your nose to the corners of your mouth. The nasolabial fold skin is tightly held down with connective tissue, and the cheek skin above becomes deflated with little underlying support. Folds form in this area, just as they do in the jowls and in the upper and lower eyelids.

3

What You Can Do about Looking Older

Currently, modern science is unable to stop you entirely from aging. However, it can help to address directly some of the visible effects of aging based on our understanding of the root causes of these problems. Antioxidant therapies, collagen-stimulating treatments, and injectable fillers are examples of technological solutions to visible aging problems dictated by our biology.

If you are at the earliest stages of visible aging (late twenties to early forties), you're just in time to look your best throughout your lifetime by taking advantage of antiaging technology right now. If you're beyond this stage in your life, you can still turn back the clock, but it will take more effort. However, it's definitely worthwhile.

CHAPTER 2

The Pause-and-Reverse Strategy

The chapters in this book discuss individual facial components or subunits and then deconstruct them into smaller parts. Details are important, but I don't want you to get lost in the fine details because the real goal is to look your best overall. To those around you (and to yourself), how you look under a magnifying glass is not critical: it's how you look in the mirror or across the table at a conversational distance. Your attitude, your warmth, your personality, the global balance of your face, your smile, and the combined physical and nonphysical impression you convey are how your beauty is judged by others.

If a specific thing bothers you about your looks or that doesn't match the apparent age of the rest of your face, then doing one thing may help your global facial balance. To remain looking youthful and healthy and to hold on to that youthful beauty require a conscious and continued effort.

You may think that moderation is the key to life. My perspective may not be popular (and it's not an opinion that sells books), but health and beauty are not about moderation. More accurately, most people's definition of moderation is not conducive to optimal health and beauty.

I would estimate that a majority of Americans think their dietary habits are balanced and moderate, but over one-third of Americans are classified as obese. It's likely that our collective perception of moderation is actually a sliding scale that has slid toward excess.

Similarly, skin-cancer rates have risen in the last twenty years, and the most common forms of skin cancer seen are directly related to sun exposure. It is proven that ultraviolet (UV) radiation is a carcinogen. This is not debatable. In addition, the majority of skin aging is directly related to sun exposure. If you use sunscreen daily, your skin will appear to look less aged over time, and you will be less likely to get the most common form of skin cancer (squamous-cell carcinoma) and melanoma. My informed opinion is that moderation is not the key, and with regard to protecting your skin, moderation is dangerous.

If you wish to look younger than your chronological age, you need to be diligent about avoiding behaviors that are known to make you look older. In conjunction with an experienced aesthetic provider, you need to be proactive in formulating an antiaging plan.

The pause-and-reverse concept is as follows:

Pause: Take steps that stop you from gathering the avoidable signs of aging.

Reverse: Then, take steps to remove some of the aging signs you have already accumulated.

Pause and Reverse Strategies

	PAUSE	REVERSE
Sunblock	●	
Retinoids	●	●
Vitamin C	●	●
Microderm	●	
Needling	●	●
Botox	●	●
Laser / Peel		●
Fillers		●
Cosmetic Surgery		●

Tools to Help You Look Younger

Today, technology and facial rejuvenation are intertwined. Creams and topical treatments have become more advanced in their formulations and ingredients. Laser and light treatments are increasingly versatile and safe. The range of treatable conditions and variety of injectable options is growing. Surgical procedures have shifted toward the minimally invasive, and surgeons now incorporate more nonsurgical techniques. The promise of the new and improved is always ahead.

Because the technological playing field changes so quickly, it's almost pointless to mention aesthetic devices by name in a print publication. Products change names, laser platforms are bought and sold by different companies, and models are modified and rebranded often. On my blog, I share my impressions of new technologies and treatments for antiaging on a regular basis. You can sign up to receive e-mails when a new entry arrives at http://drkotlus.com/blog.

I have offered my clients some mainstays in my practice for the past ten years, and I expect them to continue to be available because they produce results. The tools I'm talking about are all mentioned throughout the book, but here is a consolidated and simplified list of what products and treatments I think are important.

I talk about **sunscreen** and topical medications such as **vitamin C**, **retinoids**, and **exfoliants** with most, if not all, clients. Lifestyle modifications are even more frequently discussed (e.g., avoiding sun, smoking). **Antipigment creams** work well for dark areas of skin. Close monitoring and professional evaluation of skin growths is necessary.

Fractional resurfacing lasers (erbium or carbon dioxide) or moderate-depth **chemical peels** are the best tools we have for skin rejuvenation in lighter-skinned individuals. For darker skin types, topical agents and nonheat-based resurfacing, such as **microneedling**, are the next best thing.

Your eyes are your face's central attraction. **Botox** is the best way to reduce lines around the eyes and create some lift to the brow, and **fillers** are great for reducing mild to moderate under-eye bags. Fillers are also a great way to reduce deeper wrinkles and to plump lips and cheeks. When you have under-eye fat bags or heavy upper eyelids, **eyelid-lift surgery** works the best for the longest amount of time.

The neck is a common area of concern and a **neck lift** (or **facelift**) is a surgery that fixes the turkey waddle and jowls. Most facelifts I do are combined with **fat injections** to restore suppleness to areas of the face that have lost fat, like the under-eye area, cheeks, and temples. Nonsurgical neck tightening with focused ultrasound or radiofrequency can help, but it won't usually provide a full correction.

Pause First and Then Reverse

To look your best and youngest, you will not only need to be diligent, but you'll need to stick to a strategy that makes sense. It doesn't make sense to undergo a treatment that is a **reverse** strategy, like a laser skin resurfacing or a facelift, if you're not willing to adhere to the **pause** strategies first, like smoking cessation and routine broad-spectrum sunscreen use. The order of your approach matters if you want a healthy and sustainable appearance.

CHAPTER 3

At the First Signs of Aging

If you could pick an age when you looked your best and freeze the clock right then, when would it be? At twenty, when your skin was smooth and supple? At thirty, when you had some slight expression lines that added some character? At some point in your life, you will probably feel discordance between the way you want to look and the way you actually look. Nothing is wrong with wanting to hold on to that ideal image of yourself, as long as you are realistic and accept that tomorrow your body is going to be a day older. You can take measures within the framework of modern science that can shift your apparent age to the more youthful side of the spectrum. This can happen by adjusting your environment, your behaviors, and even the cellular structure of your body in order to extend your youthful appearance by many years.

The first signs of aging are subtle but definite. You may notice that the smile lines or "crow's feet" radiating from the outer corners of your eyes are just barely noticeable even when you're not smiling, as if they were faintly etched in your skin. You might see the same etching in a few other expression areas, including the horizontal forehead lines from raising your eyebrows, the short vertical lines between the eyebrows from scowling, and the smile lines that run vertically from the sides of the nose to the outer corners of the lips when you smile (the nasolabial creases). These fine creases are the result of the repeated expressions you've made over your lifetime. When you talk and laugh, your brain sends signals to the muscles in your face to contract in a way that conveys your emotions. The muscles shift, tighten, and relax in a pattern that transmits forces to the skin, pulling it in different directions. A fold is created at the skin-muscle connection point, and eventually the fold can develop into a fixed crease. There actually is a change in the configuration of the skin layers that represents a wrinkle.

There are other influences on when and how you develop wrinkles. Your genetics determine the basic composition of your skin and the arrangement of the muscles and fat in your face. If one of your parents has a strong smile muscle with tight attachments to the skin alongside the outer corners of your mouth, you may share similar "parentheses lines." The same familial traits can determine your body's response to external forces. Those forces include sun exposure, smoking and exposure to smoke, toxins, physical forces such as the way your face presses against the pillow at night, dryness, wind, fragrances, the foods you eat, injuries, illnesses, medications, microbes, and other organisms. Additionally, if you inherited the genes for red hair from your parents, chances are that you also inherited very light skin that may burn more easily when exposed to sunlight as compared to someone else who inherited darker skin.

The Earliest Signs of Facial Aging

Horizontal forehead lines

Under-eye shadows

Mild loss of cheek fullness

Faint brown spots

Fine blood vessels on the side of nose and cheeks

Slight heaviness of upper eyelid skin

Your apparent age—as opposed to your actual age—is partially determined by the actions you take once you identify some of these early aging signs. If early wrinkles and the effects of sun damage bother you when you look in the mirror, this is the time to act if you have not already done so. Where do you start?

Sun Protection

The most important antiaging product is sunscreen. You should have been using this throughout your life to protect your face from the damaging rays of the sun. If you didn't pay much attention to sun protection in your teens and twenties, you should start now, even if you have a darker skin type. The ultraviolet radiation emitted by the sun leads to a process called solar elastosis. This consists of degradation of collagen and elastin in the deep-skin layer called the dermis. Loss of the building blocks of the skin causes acceleration of wrinkles and sagging. In addition, the sun stimulates your melanocytes (pigment-producing cells) to make more brown spots, and the blood vessels in the skin will enlarge or dilate, causing more redness. Sun exposure and tanning beds can also cause abnormal growth of skin cells, leading to certain skin cancers. Basal cell carcinoma, squamous cell carcinoma, and melanoma can all arise on sun-exposed skin areas. Reducing your cancer risk alone is a good enough reason to be diligent about sun protection.

A 2013 Australian study published in the *Annals of Internal Medicine* followed nine hundred people from ages twenty to fifty-five to test the effects of sunscreen on facial aging. Half of them were asked to wear sunscreen every day, and the other half were asked just to follow their usual routine. After four and a half years, the sunscreen users had halted the appearance of skin aging. **UV protection can actually stop your face from aging.**

You should look for a sunscreen that offers UV-A and UV-B protection, is waterproof, and is at least an SPF 30. SPF stands for "sun protection factor," and it describes how long you can stay in the sun without getting a burn. SPF 30 means you can stay in the sun thirty times longer than if you had no protection. The American Academy of Dermatology recommends at least an SPF 15, but SPF 30 has been shown to be more effective. An SPF greater than 50 does not offer any additional benefit, and the Federal Drug Administration (FDA) has eliminated sunscreen label claims of greater than 50. It takes about the volume of a shot glass of lotion to cover the entire body. Many people forget about the lips, but you can get skin cancer there too. Some lip balms have built-in sun protection. Sun protection is important year-round, even when it's cloudy and cold outside. If you stick to only one thing in this book, this one will be the most worthwhile.

Your Environment

To some degree, you have control over your surroundings, and these surroundings definitely influence how you look. Do you spend a lot of time around chain smokers? **Cigarette smoke is linked to wrinkles.** Smokers also develop sagging upper eyelids and lower-eyelid bags earlier in life. A 2013 Ohio-based medical study of twins in which only one of the pair was a smoker showed more pronounced eye bags and wrinkles around the mouths of the smokers as compared to their healthier counterparts. It was clear to observers which of the twins smoked based on the appearance of their faces alone.

Do you spend a significant part of your day driving a car? Drivers tend to get more sun exposure on the left side of their faces, and, in fact, more skin cancers occur on the left side of the face as compared to the right side. UV rays penetrate glass, and the only way to deter them is with sunscreen or an approved UV filtering film on your car window.

Are you a stomach sleeper? Pressing your face against the pillow for the length of the night can lead to sleep lines, vertical wrinkles caused by folding of the skin. Is the air in your bedroom dry? Dry air surrounding you while you sleep can dehydrate your skin. Think about how and where you spend your time and how that may affect the health of your skin. Avoid smoke. Wear sunscreen even while driving. Place a room humidifier in your room if the air is dry. You can even find special pillows that reduce skin creasing during sleep, but there is only weak evidence that they work.

Skin Vitamins

The next measure to reduce the earliest signs of facial aging is to use a topical vitamin C product every morning. Vitamin C, a potent antioxidant, has been shown to reduce wrinkles and repair skin damage. It is a required factor for collagen synthesis, and it protects the skin from UVA and UVB damage. Using a vitamin C cream or serum at the beginning of the day will enhance the effectiveness of sunscreen while fighting wrinkles. It also inhibits the production of melanin (pigment) in the skin so it can reduce the visibility of brown spots caused by sun damage. Different forms of vitamin C are found in skin products, and not all are equal. L-ascorbic is a potent form of vitamin C derived from fruit. It is in the majority of topical vitamin-C-based skin-care products due to its effectiveness and potency. However, L-ascorbic acid is sensitive to heat, air, and light and is subject to degradation. As the product oxidizes or breaks down, it turns brown, a sign that it may no longer be useful. It should be kept in a cool, dark place. Once it begins turning brown, you should get a replacement.

Another clinically proven method of wrinkle reduction is topical vitamin A. Effective forms of this vitamin in skin products are called retinoids, including retinol and tretinoin. Vitamin A works by increasing glycosaminoglycan production in the skin, which acts to retain water and promote hydration and suppleness. Glycosaminoglycans are long chains of sugars that bind water molecules. Vitamin A also increases skin collagen, which reduces wrinkles and improves the overall thickness of the skin. Type I collagen is the major structural component of the dermis. Generally, having more collagen results in smoother skin. Topical vitamin A should be applied at bedtime, as it can make the skin more sensitive to light. It can also have a drying effect, and if you experience peeling and flaking, it may be advisable to use a lower strength or reduce the frequency of application to every other night. Some vitamin A products are combined with a moisturizer to prevent the chance of peeling and dryness.

If you only use two skin products—in addition to daily sunscreen—in your antiaging regimen, for most people a topical vitamin C in the morning and a vitamin A at night will give you the most bang for your buck. Other products are appropriate for specific skin conditions, but this is an effective combination to reduce and prevent wrinkles and skin damage.

Microdermabrasion and Microneedling

A few nonaggressive treatments can be extremely helpful at the earliest signs of aging. Microdermabrasion fits into this category. The idea behind microdermabrasion is that some form of mechanical scrubbing removes the outermost layer of skin, called the stratum corneum, which mainly consists of dead cells. The result is a smoother surface. This treatment accelerates the natural process of exfoliation. It's not a dramatic, long-term skin smoother, but, with repeated treatments, there can be some reduction in wrinkles and irregularities. It's most beneficial one or two days before a social event when you want some extra glow. Medical-grade devices use a sandblasting mechanism or a rotating burr, but some of the handheld brushes that can be purchased for home use can also do a great job. Microdermabrasion also enhances the ability of topical skin products to penetrate the skin, making them more effective. Mechanical exfoliation is only necessary about two times per week for most people. Do not confuse microdermabrasion with dermabrasion, a much more aggressive and somewhat more risky procedure only performed by physicians that grinds away skin to a much deeper level in the dermis, often to the point of bleeding. Microdermabrasion is gentler and much safer.

A slightly more invasive version of microdermabrasion is **microneedling**. This treatment involves multiple tiny needles that create tiny punctures in your skin. These needle holes stimulate collagen growth in the skin, and they create channels that let topically applied creams and serums more easily enter the part of the skin where they can be most effective.

Targeted Muscle Relaxation

Preventive maintenance can go a long way if it is initiated at the earliest signs of aging around the eyes. The movement lines, however, may require more than preventive maintenance if they are starting to become visible when your face isn't making expressions. This is especially true when it comes to the vertical lines between your eyebrows, the horizontal lines across the forehead, and the crow's feet. These lines are caused by frowning, smiling, and raising your eyebrows: the normal expressions you make during conversations. Deep lines in these areas can convey a harsh, tired, or angry look.

The best way to reduce these lines and prevent them from getting deeper is with a purified protein called botulinum toxin, most commonly known as Botox (also Dysport or Xeomin). A few injections in the proper locations will relax the frowning muscles around the eyes and forehead, soften the unwanted creases, and prevent their progression. There is a perception that Botox creates a frozen facial expression, but when it is expertly administered, the result is a natural, softer look instead of a frozen look. The benefits of Botox generally last about three to six months, and while it reduces harsh creases, it can give you a flattering lift to your eyebrows. Many people who are prone to frequent headaches find significant relief after undergoing this treatment, especially if muscle tension is their headache trigger.

Why Start Now?

Your skin is the beautiful wrapper that packages your beautiful body, and you are never too young to start thinking about wrinkle prevention. Why wouldn't you want to take care of it? I have many patients in their seventies, and I have never heard one say that he or she took too much care of his or her skin. I have heard many of them say that they wish they had protected themselves better from the sun so that maybe they wouldn't have so many wrinkles or occurrences of skin cancer.

Studies have shown that attractive people are more successful in business. A youthful face is attractive. If you start a good skin-care regimen now, you may avoid or postpone a surgery or laser procedure many years from now in addition to going further in your career.

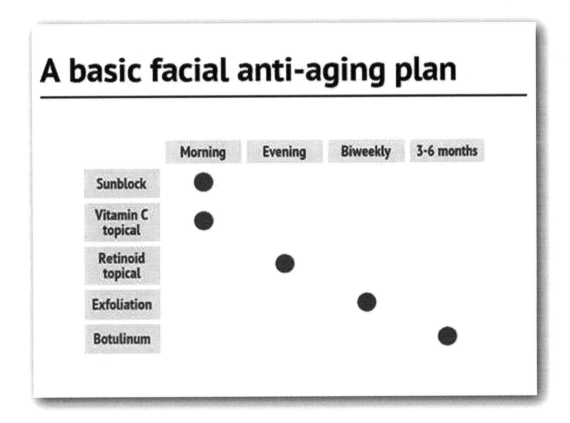

A basic facial anti-aging plan

	Morning	Evening	Biweekly	3-6 months
Sunblock	●			
Vitamin C topical	●			
Retinoid topical		●		
Exfoliation			●	
Botulinum				●

CHAPTER 4

The Five Most Tragic Mistakes You Can Make with Your Face

O K, *tragic* is a strong word. Serious tragedies are what we see on the news every night, not what happens on our faces. However, when you take a lot of care and spend your hard-earned money to look your best and something goes awry, it can feel like a tragedy. Keeping everything in perspective, here are five avoidable aesthetic "tragedies."

Mistake 1: Taking Things Too Far

One question I hear frequently when I am about to perform a cosmetic injection or procedure on a first-timer: "Now, this isn't going to make me look like [insert overdone, artificial-looking celebrity's name here], is it?"

Based on the way that cosmetic procedures are portrayed in tabloids and on gossip websites, looking artificial is a legitimate concern. The truth is that "going too far" is avoidable.

The aim of minimally invasive cosmetic procedures and cosmetic surgery is to look appropriately younger or to improve or modify an aspect of yourself that bothers you. *Appropriate* is the key word. Looking ten years younger after a facelift or five years younger after a filler injection is appropriate in relative terms. If a sixty-year-old aims to look twenty-five after a series of treatments, it's probably not appropriate, and it will most definitely look artificial. This is what we see when some aging celebrities undergo their seventh facelift, chasing after every expression line and wrinkle. Expression lines are normal. Without them, we lose some of our ability to communicate with others. Softening a deep smile line or forehead crease is reasonable if it bothers you. However, the "porcelain-doll" look should be avoided.

People who have effectively tapped into modern cosmetic medicine look five to ten years more youthful than they would otherwise, and nobody knows what they've done. Their peers comment that they look great, and their friends want to know, "What are you doing differently?"

Some social circles revere fuller-than-natural lips. There is a spectrum of tastes, and the final decision about what you wish to achieve is between you and your doctor. Keep in mind what your goals were before you did anything. Have those goals changed over the course of your treatment? Where is your endpoint? Is there an endpoint?

Tastes can also change with time. In the 1990s, it was in vogue to have a button nose or a "ski-slope" nose. It was obvious who had had a reductive rhinoplasty, and some people wanted it to be obvious because cosmetic surgery was a status symbol. Now the drive is more balanced toward natural noses that match the surrounding face. Sometimes a subtle change is powerful while simultaneously preserving your natural beauty.

Mistake 2: Neglecting the Hands and Décolletage

You've now heard many times over that sunscreen is the most important and effective antiaging product. Protecting yourself from the sun will help you avoid wrinkles, brown spots, redness, and certain skin cancers. When you're outside for any extended period, wearing a wide-brimmed hat and sunglasses in addition to sunscreen is even better. If you've been doing this for many years, the chances are that you look younger than your counterpart who hasn't been protecting his or her skin. However, have you been applying sunscreen to your neck, chest (décolletage), and hands? Nothing is more telling about your age than these often-neglected areas. Have you ever seen someone who has a smooth, youthful face and a leathery, wrinkly neck and chest? It looks as if a young head was transplanted on an older person's torso like a doll with interchangeable parts. Have you ever shaken someone's hand, and the brown spots and crepelike skin look twenty years older than the person's face?

The neck, chest, and hands may receive more sunlight than your face, especially if you're wearing a hat and sunglasses. They need just as much protection from the sun, if not more. The scary part is if you develop wrinkles, brown spots, or even worse, a skin cancer on your neck or chest, it's more difficult to treat because these areas don't heal as well as the face. As a surgeon, I can hide facial incisions within natural expression lines, but on the chest, there is nowhere to hide incisions, and scars don't heal as well. They can become thick and obvious. Lasers designed to reduce brown spots and improve skin texture can be used on the chest, but they are not as effective as on the face. This is because the neck and chest don't heal as well due to several factors. For example, the skin in these areas is thinner, and there are fewer hair follicles to facilitate healing.

When you apply sunscreen to your face using at least an SPF 30, PABA-free sunscreen with UVA and UVB protection, remember to apply it to your neck, chest, and hands if they are exposed. Definitely refrain from slathering on cooking oil and using aluminum foil reflectors as I still see some sun worshippers doing on vacation.

Mistake 3: Freezing the Forehead

Deep lines that horizontally traverse the forehead with interspersed ridges that look like road bumps may be all you think about when you see yourself in the mirror. We all develop these creases to a degree as we move our eyebrows up and down during conversation to convey incredulity, surprise, and disdain. It makes sense that many of us would like to lessen or eliminate these lines. Most clients who visit me for the first time with this concern have an idea about how they'd like to approach this: "Botox my forehead."

This is why botulinum toxin (Botox, Dysport, or Xeomin) by itself in the forehead is a bad idea: this treatment weakens the vertically oriented, paired muscles of the forehead that act not only to raise the eyebrows but also to keep them suspended. These muscles are responsible for the horizontal forehead furrows. Injecting them with botulinum toxin will soften these wrinkles, but it will also cause the eyebrows to sag. They can lose their natural arch. Softening these wrinkles will also create a heavy look to the eyebrows and potentially cause more skin to bunch or fold in the upper eyelids. The result is a smooth, frozen forehead and flat, heavy eyebrows.

A better solution is to inject the depressor muscles of the eyebrows, the ones that pull the eyebrows downward. These include the muscles between the eyebrows that create the "eleven" lines (procerus and corrugator muscles) and the muscles below the outer eyebrows that create the crow's feet wrinkles (the lateral orbicularis oculi muscles). By eliminating the downward pull exerted on the eyebrows by these muscles, the eyebrow assumes a higher, more arched position. This eliminates much of the need to excessively raise the eyebrows or furrow the forehead during conversation because the eyebrows are already somewhat higher—but not too high. Over time (the initial treatment usually lasts about three and a half to four months), the horizontal forehead lines will soften or disappear, depending on how deep they were to begin. Occasionally, the forehead can be directly treated with injections but only after treating the depressor muscles and only with sparing amounts of botulinum protein. It is much more flattering to have soft or faint expression lines across the brow with the ability to make normal movements and expressions than to have a completely smooth, frozen forehead with droopy eyebrows.

Mistake 4: Ignoring the Chin

Natural-looking beauty is almost entirely about balance. Look at a representation of the Egyptian queen Nefertiti. Her face has been widely studied for centuries as an example of ideal proportions. The upper, middle, and lower parts of her face are balanced in perfect thirds, each lending to an overall picture of perfect harmony. Most of us don't have perfect facial balance, and we don't necessarily need it. However, if one-third of our face is significantly out of balance with the other two-thirds, certain adjustments can nudge us closer to the facial relationships that allow our innate beauty to be more apparent. Having a small chin is the most common offender of horizontal facial imbalance.

A small chin causes a few other facial traits to appear "off." The nose may appear larger than it actually is. The neck can appear shorter. The jawline may appear poorly defined, and the face can appear rounder and heavier than it actually is. A small chin makes a man look less masculine and a female look less feminine. These imbalances are not the case for everyone with a small chin, but most of the time these rules apply.

What makes a small chin? For a male in profile, the chin should almost project forward from the face to the same degree as the lower lip. For a female, the chin can be a bit smaller, projecting to just behind the lower lip. From a front view, the distance from the chin to the base of the nose should approximate the distance from the base of the nose to the top of the nose between the eyebrows. A small chin may be too short from the front view or may not project enough from a profile view. It may be that your chin bone is small for your face, or it may be that the entire jawbone (mandible) is retruded or set back.

For a small chin bone, a well-selected chin implant can create a more balanced face. For some people, concerns about a large nose are discarded after achieving facial balance with a chin implant. In some situations, the perception of a large nose may still be present after balancing the chin, but a more conservative nose job may be performed than would have otherwise been acceptable.

When the issue is a set-back jawbone with a significant overbite, a jaw surgery may be in order, which can be a more extensive—but potentially rewarding—undertaking than a chin implant.

Mistake 5: Brushing Off the Maintenance Schedule

There aren't any magic pills that halt the aging process—at least not yet. When it comes to facial aging, some fixes may be close to permanent, but none of them eliminate the need for maintenance.

I hear this sentiment quite frequently: "I am tired of repeatedly getting mini treatments and creams. I want a facelift so I can forget about the other stuff." I compare this to one of my friends telling me that he wants to buy a new a car because he's tired of oil changes and car washes. Avoiding maintenance is always a mistake when it comes to both cars and your face.

Clients who are dedicated to presenting their best faces to those around them are committed to lifelong wrinkle and skin-cancer prevention. They consider facial health and beauty a part of their

25

overall health. Even if they've had an eyelid lift to help with sagging eyelid skin, they still keep up with diligent sunscreen application and moisturizer and possibly the occasional Botox treatment or skin laser to maintain a youthful skin texture. They look more radiant than they would have if they just did the eyelid lift and dropped everything else.

Some feel that they want to do this "one last thing," and then they will let themselves age. I have a good number of energetic, young-looking clients in their sixties who say, "I won't care what I look like when I'm seventy." I have many clients in their seventies and eighties who still care about their looks. The desire to look your best doesn't go away.

CHAPTER 5

Skin Maintenance and Repair

Your skin is the predominant physical interface between yourself and the world. The state of your skin sends clear messages to those around you. The leathery look is typically displayed on a sun worshipper. Deep wrinkles around the mouth may indicate a history of tobacco use. Round scars on the cheeks point to teenage acne. The condition of your skin doesn't make you who you are, but it does say something about your past. If you wish to achieve your best face, you should strive to achieve your best skin.

Skin Layers and Aging

The skin is a large and complex organ where an amazing amount of activity takes place. The outermost layer is called the epidermis, and the depths of this layer possess cells that create new skin cells. The skin-cell population is constantly turning over; old cells are shed at the surface to make room for new cells produced at the deepest portion of the epidermis. The epidermis also contains the cells that create pigment (melanocytes).

The layer below the epidermis is the called the dermis, and it works in part to support the epidermis. Here you can find oil and sweat glands, blood vessels, hair follicles, and nerves.

As we age, the skin becomes thinner, and the space between the epidermis and dermis flattens. Collagen (the major skin-building block) breaks down, and elastin fibers (responsible for skin elasticity) lose their organization. Oil glands (sebaceous glands) become less productive, thereby making the skin appear drier. Hormonal changes lead to further thinning of the skin.

The most important external factor that affects your skin is the sun. Ultraviolet (UV) light from the sun and tanning beds can cause damage in your skin's cells. Specifically, it can cause alterations or mutations in your DNA that may lead to skin cancer. It is well-proven that UV radiation is the main cause of nonmelanoma skin cancers, and it does play a role in melanoma, a potentially fatal skin cancer.

Then there is the habit of smoking and the effects of the smoke itself. The typical chain smoker has deep wrinkles that radiate around the lips. Smoking can also accentuate cheek pouches (festoons) and deep wrinkles across the entire face. Additionally, it has been shown that tobacco smoke inhibits the production of collagen. It also increases the levels of enzymes called MMPs (matrix metalloproteinases) that lead to degradation of collagen and elastin fibers. This means that the skin's basic structure is compromised by smoking.

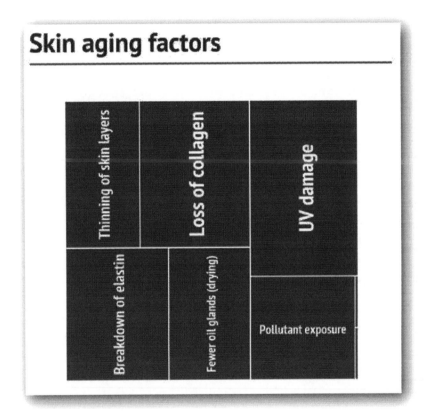

UV Protection

If you've gotten this far along in the book, you already know that using sunscreen is the most important an-tiaging strategy you can employ. Apply it liberally and frequently. Use an SPF of at least fifteen, but thirty is better. For everyday use, some excellent mineral powders and moisturizers have a built-in SPF 15 sunscreen. Physical screens that use zinc oxide or titanium oxide are excellent because they provide physical protection as opposed to chemical protection that may not be as effective and safe. In the past, the zinc and titanium sunblocks tended to make you look pasty and strange, but you can now find some products that use these ingredients in a micronized form so they appear clear on the skin. Moreover, forget about tanning beds and the mythical benefits of base tanning. If you want to get that bronze look, go for the spray-tan booth. Spray-tan technology has improved in recent years, and the good ones won't make you look like an orange. If you are outside for an extended time, wear a wide-brimmed hat. In the end, your skin will thank you for it, and you'll look younger than your friends who have been slathering on baby oil at the beach.

Your Skin Type

Finding the best skin-care program is not always straightforward. There is no simple formula. It depends on the needs and characteristics of your skin, and a chapter in a book doesn't replace a quality consulta-tion with a medical professional. However, you can get an excellent start by sticking with scientifically proven basics and matching skin products to your skin type. There are numerous ways to classify skin types. Skin can be categorized by oiliness, by degree of sun damage, by color, and by sensitivity, etcetera. Classifying the degree of oiliness (or dryness) in your skin is one of the more useful ways to choose a per-sonalized skin-care regimen. Oily skin has a tendency to look shiny with large pores and has a tendency to develop acne. Dry skin appears more dull and flaky and may feel tight after washing. You may find that your skin is somewhere between these two extremes, or it may vary throughout the year. Many of the es-sential elements of an antiaging skin-care program will work for many skin types, but extreme dryness or oiliness often requires special attention.

In the chapter "At the First Signs of Aging," I offered a basic skin-care regimen that will work for the majority of skin types. I've found that the simpler and fewer possible components in the skin pro-gram, the more likely you are to stick with it. The most basic yet effective antiaging regimen consists of a sunscreen and a topical vitamin C in the morning and a nightly retinoid—if your skin is not prone dryness. To expand on this, you should add a cleanser and a moisturizer.

Keep the Moisture In

Skin tends to get dryer with age. An easy way to keep your skin looking fresh is to keep it well-hydrated. The outermost part of the skin is made of compressed, dead cells that act as a barrier. This barrier, called the stratum corneum, is part of the epidermis, and at its best, it retains water. The moisture is kept in place with a film of oil (sebum) made by glands within the dermis.

You can maintain the skin's moisture by avoiding overwashing and minimizing harsh soaps and excessively warm water. Mild soaps or cleansers should be used with lukewarm water. Moisturizers should be applied just after washing while the skin is still slightly wet. Barrier or "occlusive" moisturizers will act to strengthen the natural oil layer of the stratum corneum and trap the water in. These work very well for people with dry skin. The main ingredients in occlusive moisturizers can include petroleum oil, mineral oil, and silicones.

Oily skin still requires moisture but may not need as much occlusion. The skin's own oil acts to prevent water evaporation. Water-absorbing or "humectant-type" moisturizers don't act like a barrier, but they enhance water absorption in the skin. The best humectants for oily skin will include ingredients such as hyaluronic acid (the same ingredient found in some dermal fillers), glycerin, or alpha-hydroxy acids. These ingredients also work for nonoily skin, but oily skin does not require the occlusive portion of the moisturizer.

Vitamin C

If you can find a good moisturizer that contains L-ascorbic acid, you can maintain water content in your skin while reducing wrinkles and minimizing the harmful effects of the sun. This way, you can use a three-in-one product so you don't have to clutter your counter with a seemingly endless amount of bottles and tubes. L-ascorbic acid is a form of vitamin C that has antioxidant properties. It fights skin aging by building up collagen while cleaning up some of the dangerous free radicals formed from UV exposure. Vitamin C also has anti-inflammatory properties; it can aid in skin repair after an injury.

Vitamin A

Vitamin A in skin products helps to build collagen and improve the efficiency of your skin's normal growth cycle. It allows new skin cells to surface quicker, which makes the skin look refreshed. Vitamin

A has been proven to reduce wrinkles and brown spots. One of the most potent forms of vitamin A for the skin is called tretinoin. It's ideal for those with oily skin because it has a drying effect and combats acne. Retin-A, a frequent favorite of acne-fighting dermatologists, is a prescription-strength form of tretinoin. Some find that tretinoin can be slightly irritating at first, but with a gradual increase in use (starting with every other day application), any initial redness or flaking usually passes. I suggest that patients apply vitamin A at night because it makes the skin more sensitive to sunlight, and it degrades when exposed to sun.

Alpha- and Beta-Hydroxy Acids

Good evidence supports the use of alpha- and beta-hydroxy acids in an antiaging regimen. These are often derived from fruits, and they act as exfoliants to help remove old skin and stimulate the growth of new skin. Glycolic acid and salicylic acid are the most common forms of these products and can be used in low percentages in moisturizing creams (5 to 8 percent) or in higher percentages in chemical peels. They can be used daily in the lotion form as a tool against sun damage and dryness. When used in the form of a cleanser, it can help with oily skin and acne.

Other Creams and Lotions

Many skin products that you find in department stores, magazine advertisements, and television commercials have no proven benefit. The truth is that advertising regulations are not very stringent, and much of the hype about skin-care products is misleading if not false. You'll often hear mentions of clinical studies in these advertisements, but they don't tell you where the study was done, by whom, and where you can read about the study. That's because they are not required to share this information with you. The clinical study showing the benefit of a cream may have been performed by the same company that manufactures the product, and the participants may have been paid to take part in the study. Obviously, there can be a conflict of interest. The best clinical studies are performed independently by researchers or physicians. If you want to investigate an ingredient in depth, search www.pubmed.com. It indexes all of the peer-reviewed medical journals and provides abstracts for most of these articles. Keep a critical eye, however, because some of these clinical studies are also paid for by pharmaceutical companies or cosmetic manufacturers. You will find excellent scientific evidence that sunscreen, vitamin C (L-ascorbic acid), and vitamin A (tretinoin) are effective antiaging products when applied to the skin.

So many ingredients are listed as the "greatest new breakthrough" in skin products that they could fill a book on their own. Some of these products may contain proven ingredients but at too low of a concentration to be effective. Others are present at the right concentration, but they are unable to penetrate the skin or they simply are unstable and degrade while sitting in the tube or bottle. Others just don't work at all.

On BB Creams

These are also known as "beauty balms" or "blemish balms" and are meant to be the Swiss Army knife of skin products. They are often promoted as an all-in-one solution for moisturizing, concealing, treating acne, and providing sunscreen. They were initially popular in Asian markets and are now universally available. The quality of these creams ranges, and while they can be great for someone "on the go," the individual components are usually not as effective as using separate products for each goal. It's difficult to pack effective combinations within one product because the concentration levels are reduced, and some components don't mix well. As with many over-the-counter products, a trial-and-error process often is required to find something that works for you.

Skin and Estrogen

For women, aging and menopause bring about hormonal decline, with lower levels of estrogen than in younger years. Decreasing estrogen levels can adversely affect skin quality. Estrogen has a protective effect on collagen. When it is absent, collagen declines, and skin becomes thinner. Systemic or topical estrogen supplementation—also called hormone replacement therapy (HRT)—can lead to increased collagen and thickening of the skin, thereby reducing wrinkles. Estrogen also maintains the moisture levels in the skin by increasing levels of hyaluronic acid within the skin that act to bind water molecules. It also helps to maintain the skin's sebum (oil) production, which prevents water evaporation. If you are perimenopausal, you may wish to discuss the possibility of a balanced, bio-similar hormone replacement plan with your doctor, particularly if you are experiencing perimenopausal symptoms. There is some debate as to whether HRT should be considered an antiaging skin treatment, but some of the evidence is compelling enough that it's worthy of discussion.

Lasers and Peels

There are as many skin lasers and peels on the market as there are protein and energy drinks. They have varying degrees of effectiveness and require varying recovery time. They treat different conditions and fall in a wide price range. How do you navigate through the array of lasers and peels? It is essential that you find a doctor you trust, either through personal recommendations from a reliable acquaintance or through your own research. The doctor should have experience with the laser or peel and have experience with the potential complications that may arise after treatment. The best way to ascertain their experience is to ask, "How many of these treatments have you done on someone of my skin type? Have you seen any complications?"

Lasers work on the skin by focusing light energy to create an effect at the skin-cell level. Often, this energy is translated into heat, and this heat creates a controlled injury in the skin. New skin cells take the place of injured cells, resulting in fresher, younger-looking skin with more collagen content. Chemical peels work in a similar way, but they use chemicals instead of laser energy to create controlled skin injuries.

Skin color is a limitation for some when it comes to lasers and peels. Darker skin types have a tendency to create more pigment after an injury, even in a controlled setting. If a laser stimulates melanocytes (the pigment-producing cells), the result is a brown patch on the skin. (See the section "Post Inflammatory Hyperpigmentation" below.) If you have a darker skin type, ask your doctor if this will limit your treatment options.

Even if you don't know the exact laser that is appropriate for you, your research should help point you in the general direction of a skin treatment based on your specific concerns.

Light-Based Treatments and Photofacials

Photofacials are common in the world of aesthetic skin procedures for many doctors because photofacials have the potential to be very effective yet are mild in terms of downtime. The photofacial treatment is also termed *intense pulsed light* because an intense burst of broad-spectrum light is repetitively flashed against the skin. These flashes of light are absorbed by the different pigments in the skin, including the red color in blood vessels and the brown color in melanin. Once absorbed, the light energy turns into heat, which can be controlled or filtered to target specific conditions. These conditions include redness (caused by fine blood vessels or telangiectasia), brown spots, acne, excessive hair, and photodamage. Multiple treatments are usually required. The results (at least for antiaging) are not as dramatic or effective compared to some of the more aggressive laser treatments, but many people don't want or need something aggressive.

A modification of intense pulsed light (IPL), called photodynamic therapy, uses a topical medication on your skin called a photosensitizer prior to light exposure. Photosensitizing agents make the skin more susceptible to the effects of light, leading to a stronger treatment. Photodynamic therapy requires a longer recovery time but can be more effective with fewer sessions and can even reduce precancerous lesions called actinic keratoses, a precursor to squamous cell carcinoma.

Nonablative Lasers

The next step beyond light-based treatments is the nonablative laser option. This is a popular procedure for those who want wrinkle reduction without substantial downtime and are willing to undergo multiple treatment sessions. *Nonablative* means that the skin's surface is not damaged by the treatment, and this usually means that swelling and redness are limited. Nonablative treatments tend to be safer than ablative lasers for people with darker skin. The nonablative lasers treat the skin by creating a controlled injury underneath the skin's surface. These injuries stimulate skin cells called fibroblasts to produce new collagen. Some of the nonablative lasers include the YAG laser (or Nd:YAG laser), the diode laser, and the erbium laser, which can also be ablative. The erbium Fraxel device is a popular nonablative laser that is effective against fine lines, brown spots, and acne scars.

A surge of devices has hit the market; these devices offer nonablative benefits but with energy sources other than laser. Ultrasound and radiofrequency energy sources and microneedles (motorized needle pens) are able to create injuries under the skin that stimulate collagen growth in a similar way as laser energy. These are also excellent rejuvenation options for patients with darker skin types.

Ablative Lasers

Ablative lasers are the workhorses of wrinkle reduction. However, with results also comes recovery time. If you have substantial sun damage and wrinkles, you have the option to undergo multiple nonablative laser treatments with minimal downtime, or you can blast them away with an ablative laser in one or two treatments. The gold-standard ablative laser is the carbon dioxide (CO_2) laser. This powerful laser creates injuries in a controlled fashion that heal in a way that allows new skin to replace old skin. It also stimulates skin remodeling that improves wrinkles, scars, and sun damage. One condition that the CO_2 laser doesn't improve is redness. However, your doctor can control the laser settings in order to target other specific conditions, including scars, wrinkles, and brown spots.

There was a time when CO_2 lasers were considered risky because they created large burn zones. These zones were at risk for infection and had the potential to leave the skin with patches of discoloration. For the most part, these issues were solved by fractionating the laser energy, as most of the newest CO_2 lasers do today. A fractional laser treatment does not injure the entire skin surface; it leaves mini islands of normal skin between the zones of ablation. By doing this, the skin recovers more quickly and with a significantly improved margin of safety. Where the old style of CO_2 laser required three weeks of downtime, the newest lasers can accomplish similar skin improvements with a single week of recovery.

Chemical Peels

Before there were lasers, the chemical peel was the sheriff in town for skin rejuvenation. These are still very popular and useful because they can be less costly than lasers and they are effective. In some situations, peels can also be used to treat a wider variety of skin types than lasers. Peels work by using a caustic chemical (usually an acid) to penetrate and peel away the outer layer of skin. Common ingredients include glycolic acid, trichloroacetic acid (TCA), salicylic acid, or phenol. The depth of the peel determines the end effect; peels can be gentle with shallow penetration, and they can be aggressive with deep penetration.

Many of the same benefits of rejuvenating laser treatments are seen with chemical peels, including improvement in sun damage, brown spots, acne, and wrinkle reduction. As with the lasers, downtime can vary significantly depending on the condition being treated and the depth of the peel. A mild glycolic peel can leave you slightly pink for two days while an aggressive phenol peel can have three weeks of real downtime. Mild peels are great as skin refreshers or as preventative maintenance and can be performed safely by an aesthetician, nurse, or physician. With the more aggressive peels that target wrinkles, it is essential that the provider be experienced. The major risks of deep peels include pigment loss (the skin can turn permanently lighter) and infections. It may be more within your comfort zone to have multiple shallow or medium-depth peels instead of a very deep one.

Brown Spots

An even skin tone looks healthier and more attractive than blotchy skin. Aside from wrinkles, discoloration is the top cosmetic skin concern that my patients voice during a consultation. What causes those brown spots to pop up as you age? There are several causes, and most of us experience one or more of them.

Sun Damage

Sun damage is by far the worst offender. Exposure to sun causes the skin's pigment powerhouses, called melanocytes, to produce pigment (melanin). Those of us with more sun damage will be left with more patchy brown areas. It seems counterintuitive, but treatments with light can reduce the uneven skin color. Intense pulsed light (IPL) can target brown areas and help to lighten them. Topical creams such as vitamin C, bleaching agents, and tretinoin can also provide some relief from the havoc caused by the sun.

Freckles

Also known as ephelides, these are concentrated areas of melanin that are most common in light-skinned individuals. They first appear in childhood and may fade over the years. They don't usually represent a serious problem, but they can be an indication that you are prone to sun damage and potentially skin cancer. As such, you should have regular checks for suspicious skin growths. Freckles can get darker when you are in the sun for a prolonged period. They can be lightened with laser treatments and chemical peels. Sunscreen will prevent freckles from getting darker during your beach time.

Age Spots

Otherwise known as liver spots or solar lentigines, these brown spots look like freckles, but they don't appear until later in life—usually in your forties or later. They used to be considered a sign of liver problems, but we now know that's untrue. Like other skin spots, these should be monitored for signs of malignancy, but they are otherwise harmless. They can be treated with lasers and chemical peels, which help to lighten or eliminate them.

Raised Age Spots

Another skin bump that crops up with aging is called seborrheic keratosis, or *seb k* for short. This brown spot has substance; it almost looks like a tiny piece of brown gum stuck on the skin. Sometimes they have a wartlike or cauliflower-shaped surface. They are not dangerous, and your doctor can remove them by simply shaving them off the surface of the skin. You may also decide just to leave them alone if they don't bother you, especially if they're in an inconspicuous area. It's a good idea to have them checked by a dermatologist to distinguish the harmless brown bumps from menacing ones, like melanoma.

Melasma (The Mask of Pregnancy)

This condition is more common in women, and it often surfaces during pregnancy. Melasma appears as flat patches of light to medium-brown discoloration, frequently on the bridge of the nose, forehead, cheeks, chin, and around the mouth. These patches are usually distributed in a symmetrical pattern. Hormones and sun exposure can stimulate melasma and darken existing patches. Some people develop melasma exacerbations after laser treatments. Low thyroid levels also can be associated with melasma development.

Melasma is one of the more frustrating skin conditions because there are no cures, but it can be treated. The types of melasma that contain superficial pigment (closer to the surface of the skin) are easier to treat, and these are often characterized by well-defined borders. When the edges of the dark patches are feathery or poorly defined, the pigment may be deeper, and the patches may be more difficult to eliminate. In most cases, melasma can be improved to some degree, and simply using a mechanical sunscreen (zinc or titanium-based) can help.

Other topical treatments for melasma include the mainstay bleaching cream, hydroquinone (HQ). It doesn't actually bleach the skin, but it blocks the production of pigment. There was some controversy a few years ago regarding HQ because it was linked to cancer when ingested by rats. Actually, the doses fed to rats were exceedingly high, and the topical concentrations used in human skin products appear safe. One caveat when using HQ is that long-term use can cause some irritation that may actually make melasma worse. It's best to use it until results are achieved and then back off. It can be started again once your skin has had some rest time. HQ has been combined with mild steroid creams by some physicians to reduce the likelihood of irritation from the topical cream. Some of the same topical treatments that help with wrinkles can also treat melasma. These include topical vitamin C (L-ascorbic acid) and retinol (tretinoin).

Lasers can work very well on the more superficial forms (epidermal) of melasma. A few treatments with intense pulsed light or fractional lasers (erbium or carbon dioxide) amazingly can lift away patches of pigment. However, there is a risk of worsening the condition because heat can stimulate a melasma flare-up. When bleaching creams are used around the time of a laser treatment, the flare-up can often be avoided or reduced. Some light chemical-peel treatments may be more appropriate for targeting pigment when you have a tendency to flare up with heat or if you are starting with a darker-baseline skin color.

Postinflammatory Hyperpigmentation (PIH)

An injury to the skin can cause a reaction resulting in melanin production, which translates as brown spots. Trauma causes inflammation, and the darker areas are referred to as postinflammatory hyperpigmentation, or dark spots, after inflammation. Some of the events that can lead to this phenomenon include acne breakouts, cuts or surgical incisions, heat from laser treatments, chemical peels, and rashes or allergic reactions to topical creams or medications. Even irritation from shaving can cause PIH.

The first approach to reducing PIH is to eliminate or reduce the inciting factor. This may include discontinuing any aggressive skin treatments, ceasing the use of irritating topical creams, and attempting to control acne flare-ups. Many of the treatments that work for melasma also help with PIH. Hydroquinone and tretinoin are mainstay treatments for these brown patches. In addition, topical steroid creams can help reduce inflammation that causes hyperpigmentation. Some regimens combine HQ, tretinoin, and steroid creams. Non-HQ depigmentation creams can also be effective.

Lasers and chemical peels should be used with caution when PIH is present. There is a significant risk of worsening the situation by creating more inflammation. That's not to say that it can't be done, but only in expert hands with some reservation.

Summary

- The most effective antiaging skin cream is a broad-spectrum sunscreen (SPF 30).
- Topical forms of vitamin A, vitamin C, and hydroxy acids are scientifically proven to reduce wrinkles and reverse signs of aging.
- Photofacials, lasers, and peels are effective treatments for wrinkles, brown spots, and redness when prescribed and performed by a trained and experienced professional.

CHAPTER 6
Your Eyes

You see the world with your eyes, the delicate and elaborate spheres that serve as an entry point for light. While your eyes help you evaluate and navigate the world, others look at your eyes to evaluate your emotions and level of energy and youthfulness. They look at your eyes to communicate and to make a connection. More specifically, people are looking at your eyelids and eyebrows, the most expressive parts of your face.

The areas around your eyes have the capability to assume a countless number of configurations based on your expressions and the state of your body. If you are dehydrated, your eyelids lose their suppleness, and they may appear sunken with excessive shadowing. If you've worked outdoors every day for years, your eyelid skin may be coarse and stretched, with deep wrinkles and folds of skin encroaching on your peripheral vision. When you are tired, the upper eyelids assume a lower position, just crossing the pupil and signaling others that you're about to fall asleep. If you are suspicious, your eyelid muscles draw the skin inward, narrowing the eyelid opening to a squint. In times of surprise, the eyelids and eyebrows pull away from the front of the eyes, creating an open-eyed stare. The permutations of eyelid and eyebrow expression are seemingly endless.

Fresh and youthful eyelids, however, are things of beauty. They are smooth but can fold and crease appropriately with your expressions. They are radiant, and they display the gleaming color of your irises. They have gentle contours that highlight the natural shape of your upper face, reflecting the unique proportions of your facial bones, muscles, and fat.

"Fresh and youthful" is a nice way to describe the perfect eyelids and eyebrows, but a better descriptor is "appropriately fresh and youthful." You wouldn't want twenty-year-old eyelids on a sixty-year-old face. That combination could look strange and mismatched. You want your eyelids ideally to look seven to ten years younger than your actual age while maintaining your own special energy and character.

Natural rejuvenation of the eyelids must take into account the multifactorial aging process, and the original eyelid shape should be considered as well. Everyone starts with a different eyelid shape that is influenced by his or her individual anatomy. No rules say your eyelids must look a certain way. Life would be boring if we looked like clones and all had the same faces.

Why Do You Have Eyelids and Eyebrows?

Aside from their function in communication, the main purpose of eyelids and eyebrows is protection. They guard your valuable eyes from injury and the elements. Blinking keeps the surface of the eye, including the window of the eyeball (the cornea), lubricated so that it can maintain clarity. Every time you blink, your tears are distributed over the front of your eyes to keep them moist. Your natural reflex to close your eyes in the wind prevents dirt and debris from landing on the sensitive surface of the eye. Even your eyelashes have a protective function; they ward off grains of sand and sense when something foreign is near your seeing organ. The brow bone is also protective; it juts out in front of the eye, ready to absorb any forceful blows you may encounter before the eyes receive any impact.

The Structure of Your Eyes

The eyelids and eyebrows are elaborate in form and function. Their shape depends on layers of tissues, including the orbital bones, the cheekbones, the fat surrounding the eyes, the eyelid muscles and tendons, the connective tissues that support and interconnect these structures, and the eyelid skin. The shapes, quantity, positions, quality, and relationships of these building blocks will determine how your eyelids look. With age, all of these components can, and usually do, change. The bones may shrink. The fat can deflate or protrude. Tendons may stretch. The skin can become thinner. The specifics of eyelid aging are very complex.

Bone

The eye itself sits inside a bony cavity called the orbit. The round rim of this bone socket is the orbital rim, which can sometimes be seen in the contours around your eyes. The upper part of the rim lends itself to some of the roundness of the eyebrow while the lower part of the rim can contribute to shadows and hollows under the eye, especially if the eyes are deep-set.

Fat

The fat compartments around the eye are important contributors to the eyelid contours. The orbital fat collection surrounds the eyeball in the orbital socket and prevents it from rattling around when you move about. The front aspects of the orbital fat can sometimes be seen as bulging pads in the upper and lower eyelids, or in people with less orbital fat, the upper and lower eyelids can have corresponding hollowing. Fat pads under the skin overlie the outside of the orbital bone to maintain support for the overlying skin. These fat pads are affectionately termed the ROOF (retro-orbicularis oculi fat above the eye) and the SOOF (suborbicularis oculi fat below the eye). The fat compartments of the cheek blend into the lower eyelid, allowing for the transition between the middle and upper face.

Muscles

The closing movement of the eyelids is caused by a broad, circular muscle that surrounds the upper and lower eyelids like a sphincter. As you close your eyes, this muscle, called the orbicularis oculus, draws the skin inward. It also creates the lines that radiate from the outer corners of the eyelids, called crow's feet. The orbicularis is responsible in part for the groove at the inner corner below the eyelid called the tear trough. This concave region is formed because the orbicularis muscle is tightly attached to the orbital bone in this area. Different muscles within the eyelids are responsible for opening the eyelids; these muscles stretch back inside the orbit. The major eyelid opener is the levator palpebrae muscle; it has a long, tendinous extension that acts like a pulley to lift the upper eyelid. This structure also contributes to the fine line in the upper eyelid called the eyelid crease. The smaller eyelid-lifting muscle in the upper lid is called Mueller's muscle. This muscle adds a few millimeters of eyelid lifting.

Skin and Connective Tissue

The eyelid skin is the thinnest in the body and has a tendency to stretch. It also tends to reveal the underlying structures with great detail. A miniscule fat pad under the skin in another part of the body would not be as visible as it is under eyelid skin. Tendons (lateral and medial canthal tendons) and connective tissue plates (upper and lower tarsus) give shape and support to the eyelids. If the tendons stretch, the eyelid itself can sag, and the shape of the eyes can change. The angle of the eyelid opening usually slopes upward as you scan from the inner corner of the eyelids toward the ears. This degree of angulation can vary due to natural variation or from stretching and sagging of the eyelid connective tissue.

Eyebrow Shape and Position

The eyebrows are dynamic structures that move while we speak and express ourselves. At rest, the contour of the eyebrow hairs differs from person to person. Women tend to have more of an arch, with the brow hairs positioned higher on the face than the underlying rim of orbital bone. Some women have a sloping curve to their brow, while others have an angular peak at the outer third. Men usually have a flatter brow that assumes a lower position. All of these variations can be considered attractive.

The Spin on Eyebrow Hair

Spinning eyebrow hair with youthful upper-eyelid fullness

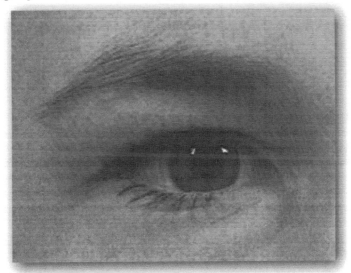

Eyebrow hair is an important aesthetic component of facial expression. Lack of eyebrow hair blunts your ability to express emotion effectively. Interestingly, your eyebrow hairs point in different directions depending on their location in the eyebrow. In the mirror, you will notice that the inner part of the brow has hair that points upward and slightly inward. If you look across toward the outer part of the eyebrow, you will see that the hair orientation rotates outward and then downward. This shift relates to the angle of the hair shafts as they exit the skin. We are accustomed to this eyebrow hair pattern, even if we don't realize it. When someone has eyebrow hairs that "disobey" this rule, we sense that something is off.

The Area between the Eyebrow and Eyelid

Some people have a plump, rounded area under the eyebrow that typically lends a very youthful look. A full under-brow area can encroach on the upper eyelid so that not much of the upper-eyelid platform is visible when the eyes are open. This is perfectly normal, and in fact, it looks good.

If you look at photos of people in fashion magazines, most of them do not have a lot of visible upper-eyelid "shelf." Still, many people seeking cosmetic eyelid surgery have the notion that more exposed eyelid is better, which is usually not the case. If the quality and contour of the under-brow skin is young, either a plump or a thin under-brow area can both be youthful and attractive. It is in many cases a misstep to go from an eyelid with not much platform exposure to one with a lot of exposure after surgery. This type of drastic change will be noticed by those who know you, and it is evident that cosmetic surgery took place. Subtle, rejuvenating changes can be created that don't scream for attention, but subtlety requires insight and restraint on your part and your doctor's part.

The Upper Eyelid and the Sulcus

There is a transition about halfway between the eyebrow and eyelid where the skin changes from thick to thin. This occurs slightly lower than the level of the bony rim. Again, this area can be plump or hollow based on how much fat is under this part of the eyelid. If there is not much fat under the upper-eyelid skin, then the upper eyelid looks sunken; this is called a sulcus. The sulcus is usually not a sign of youth. Some surgeons remove the fat under the upper-eyelid skin (the orbital fat that comes from around the eye, inside the bony socket) during cosmetic blepharoplasty (upper-eyelid lift), and it can make the upper eyelid look sunken and older. Today, most surgeons who perform blepharoplasty tend to preserve the fat behind the eyelid skin to avoid a postsurgical sulcus. However, when there is a pouch of bulging fat at the inner corner of the upper eyelid, this fat pad can be sculpted or reduced with less risk of creating an undesirable sulcus.

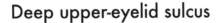

Deep upper-eyelid sulcus

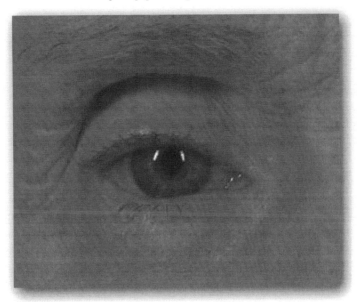

Aging of the Upper-Eyelid Skin

The upper eyelid has the thinnest skin in your body. This thin skin has a tendency to stretch. As you lose fat under the eyebrow and the upper-eyelid skin begins to stretch with age, you may start to notice sagginess or heaviness in the upper eyelids. The skin eventually hangs to the eyelashes and beyond, and the skin can obscure your peripheral sight. Stretched upper-eyelid skin also makes you look tired, more so than any other facial feature. An upper blepharoplasty (upper-eyelid lift) addresses this problem very well. For many people, the transformation after having a small strip of skin removed from the upper lids is almost magical.

Inflating the Upper Eyelid and Brow

Now that we understand that upper eyelid and eyebrow aging is predominantly a result of volume or fat loss under the skin and thinning and stretching of the skin itself, we will review the ways you can restore youthfulness to this area. When there has been a loss of fat under the skin of the eyebrow, the eyebrow-to-eyelid transition zone, and the forehead, a reinflation of the area can create a lift, just like filling a flat tire with air.

The easiest way to restore volume to a delicate part of the face is with injectable dermal fillers, which are biocompatible substances that are injected under the skin by your doctor to plump a particular area. Hyaluronic-acid-based fillers are made of a gel substance that we naturally have in our bodies. After it is injected with a small needle or a tube called a cannula (blunt-tipped filler injection cannulas can prevent bruising), your body gradually degrades it until it is gone. This can take four months to two years, depending on the specific filler used. It is highly safe because the enzyme that degrades the filler is available as an injection so your doctor can "erase" unwanted filler if needed.

A longer-lasting volume replacement can be achieved with facial implants or facial fat injections. These require some postprocedural recovery time (swelling and possible bruising will occur) but are popular and effective options.

When there is an upper-eyelid sulcus or hollowness, fillers or fat can also be added to fill the sunken space, but this can be a more delicate procedure than filling the eyebrow. Filling just along the upper rim of the orbital bone can significantly improve a sulcus. Rarely, surgeons may add fat directly into the orbital socket to fill a deep hollow space.

Brow Lifts and Upper-Eyelid Lifts

Reinflation alone may not always be enough to restore the look you used to have. When the skin is thinned to the point that it would take so much fill volume to achieve a smooth surface that the area will look overly puffy, it is advisable to do a partial fill and allow for lifting and/or skin resurfacing to take care of the rest.

The easiest form of lifting is with botulinum toxin injections. These will relax the muscles between the brows (corrugator and procerus muscles) and below the outer brow (lateral orbicularis oculus muscle) to reduce the downward pulling force of these eyebrow muscles. This allows the eyebrow to lift. A few millimeters of eyebrow lift can be both natural looking and dramatic.

Because botulinum toxin and fillers or fat injections work so well, surgical brow lifts are less common these days. Occasionally, they are still used to raise the brow to new (or previous) heights. Surgical brow lifts involve pulling up on the brow and forehead skin and soft tissues. This can be done using a long incision all the way across the scalp (bicoronal lift or hairline lift), several small incisions in the hairline with the aid of tiny cameras (endoscopic brow lift), small incisions in the temples (temporal brow lift), incisions along the eyebrow hairs (direct brow lift), or from underneath the eyelids (internal brow lift or browpexy). Once lifted, the brows are suspended with sutures, screws, implanted anchors, or bone tunnels. Your surgeon will explain each option and help you determine which one is best based on a number of factors, including the height of your hairline and your surgeon's experience with each of these techniques. Even with the lift, volume enhancement with fillers or fat may still be beneficial to achieve a natural look.

Sagging upper-eyelid skin often benefits from brow lifting because upward brow movement takes up eyelid skin slack. People with heavy upper-lid skin tend to have deep wrinkles across their foreheads. This is because they are contracting the forehead muscle to lift the eyebrows and secondarily lift some of the folded eyelid skin. Eventually, this forehead contraction doesn't do the trick, and the eyelids begin to sag visibly. This is when an upper blepharoplasty is warranted. Your surgeon can remove a strip of eyelid skin to shape the upper eyelid. Upper-eyelid sculpting can also involve manipulation of the underlying fat and muscle. Afterward, the incision is closed in a way that coincides with the natural upper-eyelid crease so that it is well-disguised after healing takes place. If you are having this done, it helps to show your surgeon a photo of your face without excessive smiling that was taken about ten or fifteen years ago so that your eyelid shape and look can be matched to what it was before.

If you use your forehead muscle to raise your brows and reduce the heaviness of your eyelid skin, then you should be aware that if you have the extra eyelid skin removed, the brows might subsequently become lower. This is because your motivation to raise your brows has been eliminated. If your eyebrows drop down after an upper-eyelid lift and you want to bring them back up, you can have a surgical brow lift, or you can have occasional Botox treatments.

Lower-Eyelid Bags and Dark Circles

Everyone hates dark under-eye circles. They can make you look like a zombie version of yourself. In certain kinds of lighting, especially overhead lights, the circles look worse. The simplest solution is an obvious one: cover up. Tinted makeup or tinted sunscreen can eliminate a large percentage of the dark area. However, why do we get dark circles?

Numerous things cause dark under-eye circles, and often multiple causes occur at the same time. Usually, shadowing from the lower-eyelid contour is the culprit. If you have any bulging lower-eyelid fat pouches or hollowness under the eyelids, the dark shadows will be more obvious. The contours of the face reflect both the skin subunits that are attached or tethered to the underlying skeleton and those that are not. A tight zone below an unattached zone causes a crease and a bulge. Imagine the tight zone is your belt, and the unattached one is your belly above the belt line. The way to improve the contour in that situation is to reduce the size of the belly or relax the tension on the belt—or both. The bulges on the lower eyelid are the orbital fat pads, and the tight area is the tear trough. The tear trough is the groove that extends diagonally from the inner corner of your eyelids alongside the nose. If you were to cry right now, your tears would roll down this trough.

Tear trough

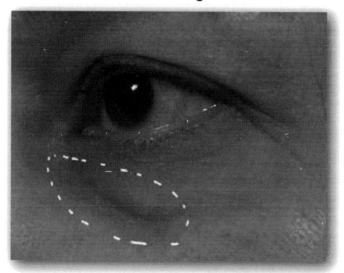

The depth of the tear trough can be reduced by adding volume with either injectable fillers or fat. **Under-eye fillers have the amazing ability to eliminate a tired appearance within minutes.** If the bulging fat is still visible after sufficiently elevating the hollows, then the fat can be reduced with a lower blepharoplasty. The fat can be approached from behind the eyelid with no visible scars or from the front of the eyelid with a thin incision underneath the eyelash line. Many surgeons prefer the back of the eyelid approach because it has less risk of causing the eyelid to sag or pull downward after surgery (eyelid retraction).

Before and after under-eye filler treatment for dark circles and bags

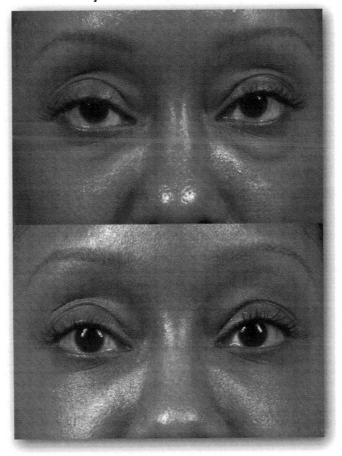

The under-eye circles can be the result of pigment buildup in the skin. You may have excessive pigment in the skin under the eyes as a response to an allergic reaction, a hormonal influence on the skin's pigment cells, or a reaction to a topical cream or medication. The first approach to this problem is to eliminate the offending cause if it can be identified. Otherwise, certain creams target pigment production and can effectively reduce these dark areas. Hydroquinone is typically the best of the bunch when it comes to antipigmentation creams, and when used with a topical retinol, it works even better.

Yet another under-eye dark-circle origin is thin skin itself. Eyelid skin is notorious for being so extremely thin that you can see right through it. What you may see are fine blood vessels (capillaries) and eyelid muscle fibers. If you can see the reddish-blue vessels and muscle through the skin in this area, then you appear to have a dark circle, possibly simulating a black eye. You can limit this phenomenon by keeping your body and your skin hydrated, thereby increasing the relative skin thickness. If you do have thin skin, you have to be cautious about having dermal fillers placed in the area because doing so may cause blue patches (Tyndall effect) or small lumps if fillers are injected too superficially. A simple cover-up cream will do a great job of disguising dark circles due to thin eyelid skin.

I created an infographic that explains the various causes of under-eye bags and how each type can be treated. You can find it here: http://www.drkotlus.com/causes-eye-bags/.

Festoons or Cheek Bags

The second set of eyelid bags are actually found at the top of the cheek. They are called festoons, which are cheek pouches that can seem fluid-filled. If you had an allergic reaction, you would accumulate fluid in this area. Some people are predisposed to these mounds, even when they are young. Festoons are another example of an unattached zone (the pouch) above a tight, adherent zone (just below the pouch where tight ligaments are attached).

Festoons can be difficult to treat. You can avoid them by limiting your dietary salt intake and sleeping with your head elevated above the level of your heart. Laser resurfacing can help firm the skin surrounding the festoon, which can reduce its appearance. Filler injections around the festoon can smooth out the surrounding contour to disguise the bulge. As a last resort, lower-eyelid surgery can improve the festoon, but it might come back.

Before and after upper- and lower-eyelid lift

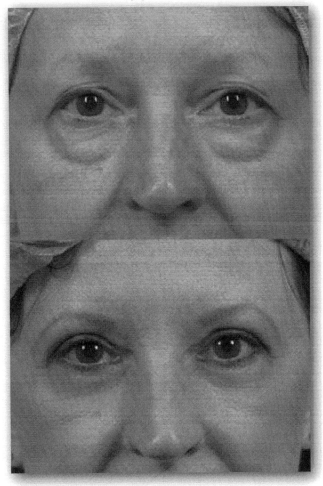

Summary

- Your eyes are the most expressive and arguably the most beautiful part of your face. When they look older, your entire face looks older.
- When the upper eyelids develop loose skin, an upper-eyelid lift is the best rejuvenation.
- When the lower eyelids have bags or dark circles, nonsurgical filler injections or surgical lower-eyelid lifts are the best means of correction. In mild cases, concealer cream or powder will hide the shadows.

CHAPTER 7
Your Cheeks and Facial Fullness

As a baby, you have round, chubby cheeks. Your baby face was full and compact. As you matured into your teens, your face elongated and expanded, but your cheeks were still relatively plump and supple. Then, in your twenties, you began to lose some facial fat. It probably wasn't noticeable. However, by the time you reach your thirties and forties, it's clear that your face is thinner in some ways. Loss of facial fat is one of the hallmarks of aging.

The Fat Compartments

The fat in your face is separated into different compartments, and some are more distinct than others. A majority of fat is found just underneath your skin in what is called the subcutaneous space. This fat blankets your face and acts as padding that translates into smoothness on the skin surface. If this layer of fat is lost, the overlying skin can sag and deflate. In the most severe cases, skin can look like a grape that has turned into a shriveled raisin.

The largest discrete collections of fat (not the fat blanket) are found in the temples, the upper cheeks (malar fat pads), the lower cheeks (buccal fat pads), and under the chin (submental fat). These fat pads add more structural support and contribute to overall roundness.

Protecting Fat and Replacing Lost Volume

Lower face changes after dramatic weight loss

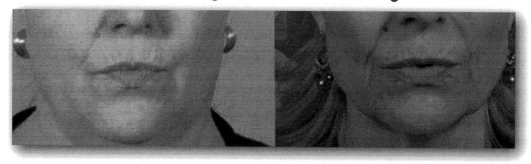

You cannot do much to stop fat from dissipating with age. There's research in the areas of stem cells and growth factors, but these methods are not yet mainstream. What you can do, if possible, is avoid dramatic fluctuations in your overall weight. A loss of twenty pounds or, even worse, a rapid gain and loss of twenty pounds can accentuate the appearance of facial deflation. Take this advice with a grain of salt, however. It's best to be healthy and at a weight that is appropriate for you.

If you've decided you'd like to get back some of the volume you've lost with age or you want to plump your cheeks before they start to look sunken, there are several options.

Injectable fillers (dermal fillers)

You can have plumping injections made from substances that are compatible with your body. These procedures are the easiest ways to restore volume and are done at a doctor's office in a matter of minutes. The fillers consist of a liquid or a gel that adds volume and stiffness wherever they are injected. Fillers placed just under the skin or in the shallow fat compartment help with wrinkles. If they are placed in the deeper fat compartments, they give structural support.

Fat injections

Your own fat can be taken from one part of your body with a mini liposuction technique and injected into sunken facial areas. This is more of a surgical procedure than dermal fillers and usually is associated with more downtime. A portion of the fat cells may not survive the transfer, and so this procedure can be somewhat less predictable than fillers. The fat cells that do survive tend to last for years. Many of my patients like the idea of fat injections because it's their own natural filler. Fat injections or "fat grafting" are most often done at the same time as other cosmetic surgical procedures like an eyelift or a neck lift.

Before and after fat injections in sunken cheeks

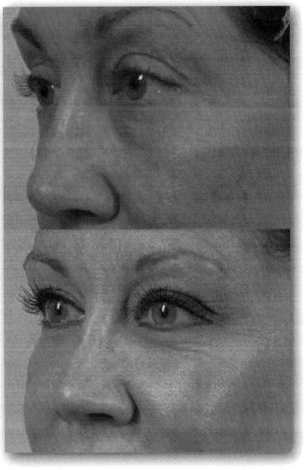

Implants

Rigid or semifirm implants can restore deep volume through a surgery that places the implants on top of a bony part of the face. Facial implants can add fullness to your cheeks and can create a stronger look to your chin as well. This approach requires the longest recovery of the three options for volumizing listed in this chapter.

Keeping It Looking Natural

One of the running themes of this book is that anything that is overdone will definitely look overdone. This also goes for filling. If you have your cheeks inflated so that the contours of your cheekbones and the transitions between the cheek mounds and the surrounding areas are blurred, you will not look natural. Your doctor should have an understanding of your goals and of the limitations of any filling procedure. It's definitely better to look only three to five years younger than to look overfilled by aiming to look ten years younger.

Summary

- As you age, you tend to lose facial fat.
- Lost volume can be restored with fillers, fat injections, or implants.
- Subtle filling is preferable to overfilling.

CHAPTER 8
Your Neck and Jawline

Your neck is the moveable pedestal for your face. Its appearance deserves mention for this reason. Ideally, a fine-art pedestal should elegantly feature the work without detracting from the work's beauty, and the same goes for your neck. It helps to frame your face, and by doing so, its appearance conveys some information about you. Your neck may provide information to others about your weight and age. It may hint at drastic fluctuations in weight. The neck skin reflects your history of exposure to the elements.

The Structure of Your Neck
Four main components contribute to the attractiveness of your neck.

Skin
The quality, texture, and tone of the skin are major factors in neck youthfulness. Major sun damage, wrinkles, and dark spots are signs of skin aging.

Fat
Excess fat under the skin of the neck or deeper in the neck under the muscles will limit your ability to have a smooth and attractive neck contour. These pouches also lend a heavy look to your face.

Muscle

The platysma muscle, a thin sheet of muscle that envelops the front of the neck, can show signs of aging when it begins to sag. It usually has a vertical seam at the center of the neck. The muscle edges become visible at this spot, and you may see vertical muscle bands in the mirror.

This platysma muscle sheet covers the deep structures of the neck, including glands and other muscles.

Bone

The chin (mandible) and hyoid bone dictate the angulation of the neck. The hyoid bone is located at the highest point of the neck where it bends. The chin is the most forward-projecting point of the neck. If there is a long distance between the neck and the chin, the neck appears to be long with a nice, sharp angle. If the distance is short, as is the case when the chin is small or when the hyoid bone is in a low and forward position, the neck angle is less favorable.

Preventing Early Neck Aging

You have probably seen commercials on television for a neck exerciser. The ads feature women who squeeze a hydraulic press between their chin and chest with admirable vigor. Sadly, they probably won't fulfill their intended goal, which is to prevent neck looseness or even eliminate it. There are no studies to support neck-strengthening exercises for neck firming. Even if you can make the platysma—the neck-shaping muscle—stronger, it won't likely be any tighter, nor will the skin and fat look better. For now, let's scratch the exercisers off the neck rejuvenation to-do list.

This may sound like a broken record, but diligent sunscreen usage does prevent skin aging everywhere on the body, including the neck. It's easy to forget to apply sunscreen on the neck and décolletage, but it will make a big difference in the end. The same skin-care regimen that you follow for your face can also maintain your neck skin. One difference is that the neck skin can be more sensitive; it may require smaller amounts of product.

Your neck will maintain its youthfulness longer if you avoid large weight fluctuations. As an extreme example, I have seen many young people who underwent bariatric surgery (stomach stapling) and lost one hundred pounds. Neck looseness (and loose skin on other parts of the body) is often an unwanted result, but the health benefits of the massive weight loss are definitely worth the negatives in the vast majority of cases. Even a twenty-five-pound weight loss can leave some people with loose neck skin. A relatively stable weight can lend stability to the structure and shape of your neck.

Poikiloderma—Say What?

Poikiloderma is a strange word that describes a common situation. It's the sun damage that occurs on the neck and chest that looks like redness with scattered brown spots. The skin in this area becomes thin, and small blood vessels called capillaries become visible beneath the skin and cause it to appear red. The best way to treat this problem is to prevent it before its appearance becomes bothersome. Once again, sunblock is your best friend. Once you have poikiloderma, you can reduce it with laser treatments. Intense pulsed light (IPL), pulsed-dye lasers, and fractional resurfacing help. These treatments are administered by doctors experienced in laser skin therapies.

Neck Bands

For some, the first indication that the face is starting to sag southward is the small band, or *wattle*, under the chin. Sometimes this appears as a single band, and other times there are two bands. These represent the central portion of the platysma muscle. The thin muscle sheet that spreads over the neck and just over the jawline is the muscle you use to pull down the outer parts of your mouth when you floss your teeth. When you flex this muscle, the neck tightens like a trampoline. If you see the central bands when you relax the muscle, there is a lack of connective tissue support or a lack of facial fat that was previously keeping your facial muscles taut and in place.

The most mild, early bands can be treated without surgery. A series of botulinum treatments (Botox) in the bulk of the muscle band will promote either localized muscle atrophy or shrinkage as appropriate. If the substance of the muscle band is small, it may lift or appear less obvious. Doctors have used this type of "injectable lift" along the jawline at the upper edge of the platysma muscle with some modest results. The term *Nefertiti lift* is sometimes used to describe botulinum treatments that improve the jawline. Doctors sometimes use focused energy, such as ultrasound, to help tighten the neck muscle without surgery. The results are not typically dramatic, but they can be helpful if your neck isn't especially loose. Other nonsurgical treatments for these muscle bands are usually not helpful. Skin tightening procedures applied to the neck aren't able to tighten enough to support a sagging muscle.

A surgical procedure called platysmaplasty is the best long-term solution for neck bands. A platysmaplasty is similar to a neck lift, and it can involve a few steps. If there appears to be extra platysma muscle, the muscle is trimmed. The loose muscle edges along the middle of the neck are usually sewn together with thin stitches. The muscle can be oversewn in multiple layers, like a corset (hence the term *corset platysmaplasty*). This smooths out the neck and improves the neck angulation by cinching the muscle. The muscle may then be released beneath the corset stitches, termed a back-cut. This can help eliminate bowing of the muscle and reoccurrence of the bands. Excess fat may also be trimmed from beneath and/or above the platysma to give more shape to the neck. Other neck-shape modifications include trimming overly bulky digastric muscles (a muscle that is deep to the platysma) and trimming the submandibular glands (a saliva gland that sits under the jawbone) if they are bulging. Platysmaplasty is most often performed at the same time as a lower facelift, which tightens the jawline and improves loose skin and muscle in the lower part of the face.

Before and after platysmaplasty (with a facelift) for neck bands

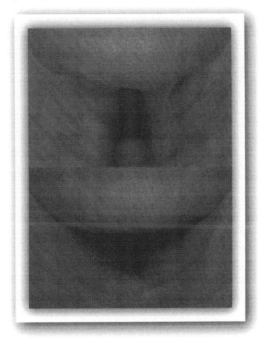

Neck Pouches

You may have a bulge or a thick area just under your chin that is accentuated with weight gain. This could be a collection of fat cells. A heavy-looking neck frames the face in such a way that the face itself appears to be heavy. A small amount of fat removal with liposuction can dramatically alter a heavy appearance and improve the contours of the neck and jawline, but there are a few caveats.

If muscle bands are present, neck liposuction can make these more noticeable. Essentially, by removing the fat that blanks the sagging muscle, the bands are exposed. This is mostly the case in people over the age of forty-five.

A newer treatment for under-chin fat (double chins) is the mesotherapy injection. A medicine in liquid form is placed under the neck skin with a needle, and it works by gradually dissolving the fat cells. The medicine (usually deoxycholic acid) disrupts the wall of the fat cell. Mesotherapy requires multiple treatments (usually three to six), and each treatment causes swelling and discomfort that can last a week. It is usually not as effective as liposuction, but it's an option if you wish to avoid surgery.

If the hyoid bone that defines the highest point of the neck is sitting in a low and forward position, no amount of fat sculpting will create a sharply angled neck. The underlying anatomy dictates the maximum benefit that can be obtained by shaping the surface tissues.

Bulges on the Side of the Neck

There are saliva glands just underneath the jawbone on both sides of the neck. These glands are the same ones that enlarge when you are sick. They are called the submandibular glands because they are below the bone called the mandible. The purpose of these plum-sized glands is to contribute to the production of saliva. They can drop down with age, which can cause them to be more noticeable. They also tend to be more noticeable in thin people who have little fat covering the glands.

Submandibular gland bulges can be improved with surgery that removes a portion of the gland. In most cases, I feel that the risks associated with surgery for enlarged glands aren't worth the reward.

Jowls

These areas of sagging are located just above your jawline on either side of your chin. They happen because you have lost fat in your face (deflation), your muscles and connective tissues have become looser, and gravity has taken a toll on these areas.

Early, mild jowls can be disguised with filler injections just in front of the jowl, creating a smoother jaw contour. These injections fill in the divot just in front of the sagging jowl. Some skin tightening procedures can also improve a mild jowl. However, when you have serious jowls, a facelift may be the only way to get rid of them.

Facelifts

The neck and the neck muscles are a visual and anatomic continuation of the lower part of your face. It then makes sense that a facelift addresses both the neck and the lower face. *Facelift* is a broad term that covers a variety of procedures and versions of those procedures. Usually the term facelift is used to mean *lower facelift* and describes a lifting procedure of the jawline and neck. Lifting of the eyelids and brows can be done at the same time as a facelift but are not necessarily included in a traditional facelift.

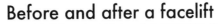

Before and after a facelift

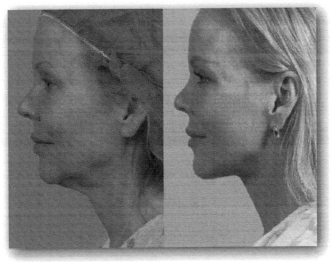

Variations on the facelift procedure are numerous. On television and in magazines, you hear and see phrases like mini facelift, liquid facelift, lunchtime lift, S-lift, and other branded nomenclature. I have even seen some moisturizing creams that are called a "facelift in a bottle." The nonsurgical or liquid facelifts usually involve injectable fillers to restore volume, botulinum toxin to relax muscles causing wrinkles, and laser procedures to improve the skin quality. These procedures work very well and can produce dramatic results but do not always do a good job of eliminating jowls or neck bands, which usually require a surgical approach.

Mini facelifts are surgical procedures that use smaller incisions and less aggressive steps than a "full facelift." They tend to work well for people in their forties or fifties who have early signs of aging and for those who don't have heavy necks and jowls. There are many variations on mini facelifts, but they typically involve an incision around the ear to allow the surgeon to access the facial muscles that are tightened during the procedure. The incision may start near the sideburn and end below the earlobe or behind the ear. In most cases, a mini facelift works very well for the jawline and jowls but not as well as a full facelift for the neck.

A **full facelift** also has many variations, but it generally uses incisions around the ear and under the chin to tighten the jawline and the neck. These incisions are designed to hide in the natural architecture of your face. They are placed in the hairline, along creases in the ear, and in the crease under your chin. They usually heal within a few months and resemble a thin line that is barely perceptible. It is impossible to predict how each person will heal, but even if the scar line becomes slightly thick, it can usually be treated with laser or injections to achieve a nicely disguised, thin line.

The muscle tightening done under the skin is the workhorse of the facelift. The cheek muscle in question is the SMAS (superficial musculoaponeurotic system), which is a thin but strong network of connective tissue that facilitates facial expressions. Some surgeons will simply use stitches to tighten the muscle. Others will remove a strip of muscle and stitch the ends together to create firmness. Some will tunnel deep under the muscle (deep-plane facelift) and tighten up the entire layer to lift the face. All of these techniques can work well.

Excess skin is removed around the ear in a facelift. However, the removal of skin alone is not enough to lift the face. Skin is not a strong support structure, and it will eventually stretch back out. The muscle tightening does the major lifting, and the skin removal takes up the slack but does not create the lift.

A Natural-Looking Facelift

A natural-looking result is the goal of the modern facelift surgeon. A windswept look is passé. There are a few ways to avoid an unnatural result.

If your face is thin, meaning you have sunken cheeks or you simply lost weight in your face over the years, then it makes sense to restore volume in these areas. Usually, lifted and filled looks better than just lifted. This is done with fat transfer techniques. A mini liposuction is done in one area of the body, and the harvested fat is injected under the skin in the cheeks, temples, or wherever needed. Other ways to restore volume are with cheek implants and dermal fillers.

If the lower part of the face is rejuvenated with a facelift but other parts of the face also could benefit from rejuvenation, it is favorable to address them all at the same time to avoid a mismatch in appearance. Loose eyelid skin and sun-damaged skin are treated during a facelift, when necessary, with an eyelid lift and skin resurfacing. You also have the benefit of minimizing the downtime of multiple procedures if you bundle them.

———

Summary

- The shape and youthfulness of your neck are mainly determined by the condition of your neck skin, fat, and muscles.
- Neck skin needs to be protected from the sun to prevent sun-induced aging.
- Mild neck aging can be treated with nonsurgical methods, including Botox injections or focused ultrasound.
- Under the age of forty, liposuction may be the best way to improve your neck shape if you have excess under-chin fat.
- If you are over the age of forty or when muscle bands are noticeable, a neck lift is often required to tighten the neck.

CHAPTER 9

Your Lips

Next to the eyes, your lips are a focal point of your face when you converse with others. The lips are delicate, expressive, and sensual. A youthful, attractive lip on a woman's face relies on plumpness, natural curvature, and structural definition. Pretty lips also lack wrinkles in the surrounding skin. Men's lips don't need to be as round and full to be deemed attractive, but exceedingly thin lips are considered less desirable.

As you age, your lips become smaller and can start to look thin and deflated. If your face is youthful-looking but your lips are almost nonexistent, a lip enhancement gives your face balance.

Interest in lip aesthetics reached a pinnacle in the early 2000s due to the widespread availability of injectable treatments. Images in popular culture began to reflect the rise in lip enhancement procedures, and the perceived ideal for lip size and shape shifted to a larger-than-natural baseline. As the requests for "Angelina lips" poured in to cosmetic physicians' offices, almost cartoonish examples of overdone lip enlargements were featured in exposés of cosmetic surgeries gone wrong on television and in magazines. Some of these sad cases involved injections of unsafe substances (including industrial silicones) that left behind significant deformities. Since then, full lips have remained in vogue, but most cosmetic providers have settled on a more balanced goal of inflated lips that don't go over the top.

The Structure of Your Lips
The foundation of a balanced lip enhancement is an understanding of the lip structure. The most crucial aesthetic elements include the vermillion border or white roll, the Cupid's bow, the oral commissures, and the overall lip volume and contours.

The Vermillion Border
The fine whitish line that separates the pink mucous membrane of the lip from the surrounding skin is called the vermillion border or white roll. Volume or color enhancement in this line creates highlights and definition around the lips and can minimize the appearance of wrinkles around the lips.

Cupid's Bow
The dip in the center of the upper lip is said to resemble the bow of Cupid. The two peaks of the bow continue upward to form the philtral columns, the ridges that vertically travel from the upper lip to the base of the nose.

Oral Commissures
The oral commissures are the outer corners where the upper and lower lips meet. If these are downturned, the mouth appears to frown. Alternatively, upturned commissures are associated with pleasantness.

Natural Lip Contour
The lips have natural curves, usually two elongated ovals for the lower lip, with a subtle dip in between. The upper lips often have indentations at the highest points of the two lower lip bulges. These curves can differ among people. Loss of lip contour due to too much filler creates an unnatural appearance, sometimes referred to as "sausage lips" because the curves are lost and the lips look like two stacked hot dogs.

Lip Plumping

Lips can be made larger, or they can be made to appear larger without actually changing their size.

Makeup

Lipstick and lip liner can create amazing illusions of larger and more defined lips. Color alone makes the lip look bolder and larger. Liner of a slightly different color around the lips adds highlights and definition. Lipstick is the most common form of lip enhancement worldwide.

Lipstick with mucosal irritants creates temporary lip plumping by increasing blood flow to the area. Capsaicin (found in hot peppers and pepper spray) is a common lip-plumping ingredient. These products tend to work for a few hours at a time.

Filler Injections

This is the most popular way to plump the lips for months at a time. Hyaluronic-acid gels are most often used because of their high safety profile. This semifirm gel is injected around the lips (vermillion line, under the lip mucous membrane, and in the philtral columns) to add volume. Fillers can be dramatic or subtle, depending on how they are performed and how much volume is added. These fillers usually last for a period of six to twelve months after each treatment.

Longer-lasting fillers are sometimes used to achieve a more permanent result, but these are also associated with more risk. If lumps occur, there are few options to remove them other than surgery.

Before and after lip-filler injection

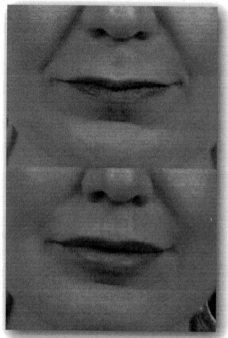

Fat Injections

Fat from another part of the body can be placed in the lips using small amounts at a time. These treatments tend to produce less predictable results than filler injections because some of the fat cells are reabsorbed by your body. The results, however, can be long lasting and often quite natural looking.

Lip Implants

Implants can be placed inside the bulk of the lip to add volume. Surgeons use nonreactive materials that are compatible with the body, including silicone, Gore-Tex, and acellular dermis (AlloDerm). Implants are not as popular as injections because injections are perceived as being safer and easier to perform.

Surgical Lip Lifts

Surgery can do things that just adding volume can't do. It can shorten the distance between the lip and the nose by removing a strip of skin. It can pull the lips outward by removing skin next to the lips. It can also push the lips outward by advancing the mucous membranes inside the lips. Surgery works well, but it often leaves scars behind. These scars can be hidden in existing creases and disguised with makeup.

Summary

- Don't aim to make a drastic change to your lips. If you do so, it will be obvious.
- A plumping procedure should keep your natural lip shape as the blueprint for the result.
- Subtle additions and gradual changes are the best way to have flattering lips instead of flapping lips.

CHAPTER 10

Your Nose

The look of your nose may not be the first thing you think of in a discussion of facial aging, but it is a major factor when it comes to facial beauty. The most important function of your nose is breathing. More accurately, your nose must allow the passage of air to your lungs while acting to warm and moisturize that air. Second to being a working nose, your nose has an aesthetic function. It should contribute to the overall balance of your face and maintain reasonable proportions, and it should not detract from your other attractive facial features. In other words, your nose needs to breathe, and ideally, it should not be too conspicuous. It's been said that a nice nose doesn't draw attention to itself, allowing the beauty of the eyes to take center stage.

Unusual or asymmetric noses are not necessarily unattractive. Look at a handful of Hollywood actors and actresses. You'll notice features of their noses that you haven't detected before. They may not be straight, or they may have a dent in the side or a nostril that flares more than the other does. It's OK if the lines of the nose aren't picture perfect. Sometimes a completely perfect nose looks unnatural or "done." The nose should fit the surrounding face, and variations are interesting and can be attractive.

The Structure of Your Nose

The nose is a chambered organ that is built somewhat like a house. It has a roof, a floor, and rooms. It's constructed from layers of tissue including skin, bone, cartilage, and mucous membranes. All of these components are necessary to maintain the integrity and function of the nose, and the relationships between these structures determine the shape of the nose.

Bone

The nasal bone makes up the roof of the upper third of the nose, just between your eyes. This bone is a continuation of some of the bones around the eye and has two halves that join like a triangular roof on a house.

Cartilage

Much of the nose structure is formed from semirigid cartilage. Cartilage lends the shape to the lower two-thirds of the nose. The middle third of the nose is formed by the upper lateral cartilages, which are essentially shaped just like the nasal bone, just softer. The lower third of the nose, or the tip, is formed by the lower-lateral cartilages, which are domelike structures with side wings. These create the ball at the tip of your nose and the flaring section of your nose around the nostrils.

Septum

In the nose/house analogy, your nostrils are the doors that allow entrance to the two rooms of your nose, and the septum is the wall that separates these two rooms. The top of the septum is the bridge of your nose, and it extends vertically downward to the floor of the nose. The front half of the septum is made up of cartilage, and the back section is bone. The septum supports the roof of the nose and gives it height. Its position helps to determine if your nose is straight or crooked. The septum is covered by a mucous membrane, as is the entire inside of the nose.

Skin

Obviously, the outer covering of the nose is skin. The nose skin can be thick or thin, oily or dry, and smooth or bumpy. The characteristics of your nose skin will affect the apparent size and contour of your nose.

Your Nose Shape

The way your nose looks is entirely dependent on the shape and relationships of the anatomic parts of your nose. Each subunit lends to the overall appearance like pieces in a puzzle. Changes to these subunits can be made to modify the global look of the nose or to refine a specific feature.

You may dislike the shape of the tip or a bump on the top of your nose. These are the two most common issues that lead people to seek a cosmetic nose consultation.

The Bulbous Tip

W. C. Fields is the archetype of someone with a bulbous nasal tip. He was a performer and comedian in the 1930s with the skin disorder called rosacea. It can cause thickening and redness of the skin due to overactivity of oil glands and small blood vessels. When it happens on the nose, it can produce a round-looking ball on the tip. In W. C. Fields's case, alcohol exacerbated the problem; alcohol worsens rosacea. Round noses caused by rosacea can be treated by avoiding aggravating factors (e.g., sun and alcohol), by applying certain topical creams (such as metronidazole cream), and in severe cases, by using carbon dioxide laser treatments.

A round or boxy nasal tip is most frequently caused by the shape of the cartilages of the lower third of the nose (i.e., the lower-lateral cartilages). If the width of these domed arches is large or flared, the tip of the nose assumes that shape. The most effective way to refine or reduce a round, ball-like nasal tip is with surgery. It requires removal of some of the width of the thick lower-lateral cartilages and/or internal stitches that bring these arches closer together.

A Nose Hump

A hump on the top of the nose often makes people feel that their nose is too large. It can also detract from the femininity of the female nose or add coarseness to a man's nose. Several configurations give the appearance of a hump.

If the nasal bone or the top of the nasal septum has too much height, then the nose appears to have a bump. The septum is most commonly responsible, but sometimes there is a combination of bone and septum causing the problem. The most direct way to address this concern is by trimming the top of the septum and reducing the height of the bone with a rasp or chisel during rhinoplasty surgery. (It sounds more gruesome than it actually is.) A nose hump can also be caused by a droopy tip of the nose; this creates a convex slope to the nose when viewed from the side. The nose may not actually have a hump, but it can appear to have one until the tip is turned upward during rhinoplasty.

A deep recess at the point where the top of the nose meets the forehead will also create the illusion of a hump. In this situation, nonsurgical rhinoplasty is an option. Nonsurgical rhinoplasty uses injectable fillers (including hyaluronic-acid gels or hydroxylapatite gel) to add bulk strategically to portions of the nose. If there is a depression at the top of the nose, it can be filled with an injection that can mask a hump nicely. In the proper scenario and with an experienced injector, a nonsurgical rhinoplasty can be quite effective and flattering.

Nose-filler injection to disguise a hump

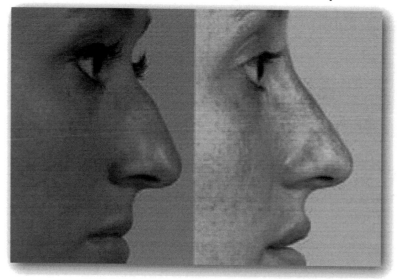

Nose Fillers

Fillers work well to disguise a nose hump, but they can also be used to improve asymmetries or to add height. Some noses that appear wide are actually lacking height along the top of the nose. When filler injections are performed along the top ridge of the nose, the added height creates the appearance of a narrower nose with more definition and highlights from light reflections. Nose fillers are quite popular in Asia for this very application. Asia is a hotbed for minimally invasive cosmetic surgery procedures, and nasal filler fits the bill because it can produce a dramatic result without surgery. The results last for about a year, which can aid in determining if a more permanent surgical procedure is warranted. It acts as a trial period in a sense.

The Crooked Nose

A nose with a curve or a bend is more common than you might expect. Asymmetric facial features are a rule rather than an exception. One of my cosmetic surgery mentors used to tell his patients that "the breasts are sisters, not twins," referring to the high prevalence of asymmetry. The same dictum holds true for all paired structures on the body.

A twist or bend to the nose is usually caused by a twisted or bent nasal septum. Some people use the term *deviated septum* to describe a curved septum, but technically, curves and deviations are different. A deviated septum is just shifted to one side, not necessarily curved. A twist can also be caused by nasal bones that are off to one side or paired nose cartilages that are larger on one side. Correction for these issues involves surgery to rearrange the bent or uneven cartilage or bone. A section of cartilage can be removed, or a bone can be repositioned to straighten out the lines of the nose.

A curvature that is visible on the outside of the nose might mean that the inside airway is wide open on one side of the nose and too narrow on the other side. Breathing may improve when a crooked nose is straightened.

What Makes a Nose Look Fake

Overdone noses are easy to spot. They can be too sloped, too pinched, and too narrow. Plenty of people are born with sloped button noses, but these noses usually fit with the rest of the face. A tiny nose doesn't usually match a face with larger, coarser features. The most unnatural-looking noses after rhinoplasty are overreduced or their characteristics have been changed too much. Most people think of Michael Jackson's nose when rhinoplasty comes up in conversation. His nose was clearly overreduced to the point that it was collapsing, and his airway was compromised. Michael was an unfortunate case of someone who probably felt his nose was never good enough, no matter how many times he underwent surgery. He's also probably an example of someone with body dysmorphic disorder, a true psychiatric disease classified as an obsession with a perceived physical defect. Sadly, it can lead to an obsession with cosmetic surgery and, ultimately, serious depression. Most people who undergo rhinoplasty do not suffer from body dysmorphic disorder, but those who have this problem require extensive counseling before any consideration of going under the knife (which ultimately may not be advised).

Summary

- Your nose doesn't have to be perfectly symmetrical or very small to be attractive. It is important for your nose to fit your face.
- Nose surgery (rhinoplasty) reshapes the nose by modifying the cartilage and bone.
- Fillers can be used in only some situations to reshape the nose without surgery.

CHAPTER 11

Home Remedies

We've all received advice, welcomed or unsolicited, from friends, family members, and daytime television hosts about how to look better with household items or some bizarre potion. Everybody and his or her hairdresser seem to have an ancient remedy for what ails you. In my office, I think I've been asked about all of them. A patient once inquired about frog urine, asking if it cures acne. No kidding.

It's not always easy to distinguish truth from myth when it comes to these practices. In several instances, there is a real basis for home remedies. In others, the attraction is being let in on a "secret" that circumvents the commercial cosmetic industry. Perhaps some harmless items can evoke a placebo effect, and some remedies may simply work for some of us but not for others.

Below I share my impressions on the fifteen most popular home remedies used for antiaging, eye bags, and cosmetic-surgery recovery.

Home remedies

Witch hazel

Coconut oil

Bromelain

Egg

Honey

Mud

Sugar

Arnica montana

Preparation H

Green tea

Cucumber

Zinc

Olive oil

Adhesive tape

Lemon juice

Eye Bags

Preparation H

This popular hemorrhoid cream has also become popular for under-eye puffiness. The active ingredient is phenylephrine, which shrinks blood vessels. This effect could temporarily reduce the visibility of prominent eyelid veins, but it won't do much for the puffiness. You also risk developing irritation or a rash when placing a product designed for, well, a "lower part" of your body on a sensitive area like the lower eyelids.

Witch Hazel

Also known as *Hamamelis virginiana*, this powerful astringent agent works on the surface of the skin to cause some contraction. It can reduce the visibility of pores and make the surface feel tighter. As with Preparation H, the results are not long-lived. In addition, if you have dry skin, this agent can make the skin drier. Avoid contact with the eyes. It won't take care of major bags, but it could provide a minor beauty boost in the way of smoother under-eyes for a few hours.

Cucumber Slices

Everyone knows about placing cool cucumbers over the eyes as a beauty treatment to reduce eye bags. Cucumber slices are not special, but they fit nicely around the rim of the orbital bone. They have high water content, so they maintain a cold temperature after coming out of the fridge. The same goes for a frozen steak applied to the recently acquired shiner of the leading man in some old films. Some people do the same with the curved back of two metal spoons that were stored in the freezer. Any type of cool compress will work in the same way to reduce blood flow to the area, possibly reducing some puffiness. I recommend a bag of frozen peas to my patients after eyelid surgery as it molds nicely to the contours of the face. And sometimes cold just feels good.

Green-Tea Bags

These have been more in vogue recently than cucumber slices, mostly due to the antioxidant hype surrounding green tea. Many creams contain antioxidants to help reduce sun damage and skin aging. The antioxidants found in green tea are called polyphenols. Are polyphenols effective when placed on the skin in a bag of green-tea leaves steeped in water? Currently, no studies have determined if this approach is effective, but there is some evidence that green-tea-derived polyphenols protect against ultraviolet sun damage and improve skin elasticity. As long as you don't burn your eyelids, there is probably minimal risk.

Antiaging

Adhesive Tape

The idea of using adhesive tape on your face may evoke images of children playing with Scotch Tape to fashion gruesome, zombielike expressions with upturned, flattened noses and eyelids cinched to their cheeks. However, there are two ways to use tape to combat facial aging that don't make you look like a zombie.

There's an old theater trick in which strips of adhesive (sometimes called theatrical tape or instant facelift tape) are attached to the skin in a few strategic locations (often under the earlobe and just under the sideburn) and fastened just in front of the hairline to simulate a neck lift or a cheek lift. It can even be used on the forehead as long as your hair is long enough to hide the tape. I've seen this used by people who were not candidates for a surgical facelift because of other medical issues.

I once met a client who used tape to pull up her eyebrows during a consultation for Botox. I didn't catch the tape because she was disguising it with a dense wig. She came back a few weeks later without the tape and said the Botox didn't work. The eyebrows were definitely in a lower position. My keen staff member, who had noticed the theatrical tape on the client's previous visit, pointed out that she wasn't wearing the "brow-lifting" tape on the second visit. The client admitted to the tape lift and said she was able to get free Botox from other providers with this ruse. She left the office amicably but embarrassed.

The second beauty application for tape is to apply it before bedtime to a furrow or wrinkle. Using your fingers, flatten or stretch any facial wrinkle and cover with tape to maintain the flatness. Clear, stiff surgical tapes work well, but some people use ordinary Scotch Tape. The idea behind this remedy is that the tape prevents furrowing during sleep, which is how we spend at least one-fourth to one-third of our time. This "wrinkle splinting" may reduce the severity of deep lines and prevent new ones from forming, especially if you are prone to being facially expressive during slumber. There currently aren't any scientific studies showing how effective this technique is, but the concept makes some sense, even if it makes you look funny in your sleep.

Mud

Facial masks consisting of mud or clay are used to tighten skin, remove impurities, and reduce acne. Do they actually work? Mud makes the facial skin feel tighter because it draws water and oil from the skin. Dehydrated skin feels tight, but this doesn't mean your face looks tighter. Because mud masks reduce oiliness, they can help with overactive oil glands that lead to acne. There is evidence that certain types of mud have antibacterial properties (such as Dead Sea black mud) that can further improve acne. It is not evident that mud alone actually reduces wrinkles, but often other agents are added to store-bought mud masks that can provide other benefits.

Egg

Chicken eggs are often touted as natural facial-smoothing agents. Some advocate using the white as an astringent followed by the yolk as a moisturizer. While there may be some basis for these claims, there is no evidence that eggs are any better than other astringents and moisturizers that don't carry the risk—however minor—of salmonella colonization.

Olive Oil

Save it for cooking. Natural oils are easy to find in your kitchen cabinet, but they don't necessarily belong on your skin. One study showed that four weeks of twice-daily applications of a few drops of olive oil to the arm skin resulted in a breakdown of the outer layer of skin and the development of redness. It's also known to be comedogenic; that is, it has the potential to cause acne flare-ups in some people. Stick to other less irritating plant oils or moisturizing products that are tested and formulated to penetrate and hydrate your skin.

Coconut Oil

Coconut oil on the other hand has been shown to be safe and effective as a moisturizer. The same goes for aloe. The benefit of pure plant-based oils is that they may be less likely to cause allergic reactions because they lack many of the chemicals and fragrances found in commercial products.

Honey

Honey has been used for ages as a topical skin agent for wound healing and beauty. This is largely due to its innate antibacterial and antifungal properties. However, unless you are using medical-grade honey, there can be bacterial contamination in store-bought honey products. The bottom line is that if you have a wound, you should see a doctor or a wound-care specialist and follow his or her advice, which most likely won't include honey dressings. Save that for your lunch salad. If you find yourself stranded in the wild with a cut, then you should consider this remedy. The beauty benefits are not very convincing.

Lemon Juice

All citrus fruits are acidic, and this gives them some properties that can affect your skin. As with the commercially available alpha-hydroxy acid topical products, lemon juice can lighten the skin and reduce signs of photoaging. The acidic content of lemon juice exfoliates the outer-skin layer, which increases the skin-cell turnover and helps to lighten dark spots. A simple method is to apply a thin layer once or twice daily and leave it on the skin for at least five minutes before washing it off. Commercial products, however, tend to be more reliable because they can deliver a more consistent and controlled product.

Sugar Scrubs

Brown or white sugar is a popular ingredient in facial and body scrubs because the texture creates a mechanical exfoliation of the skin surface, just like microdermabrasion. These treatments can help the skin feel smoother, but there is a risk of overdoing it. Too much scrubbing will leave the skin red and irritated. The skin doesn't need aggressive exfoliation on a daily basis. Once or twice a week at most should be sufficient because the outer layer of skin is necessary to help retain moisture.

Postsurgical Recovery

Arnica

Arnica, or *Arnica montana*, also named wolf's bane, is an herb that has been promoted to reduce bruising and swelling after surgery. The vast majority of preparations are homeopathic, which in itself deserves an explanation because use of the word is so widespread.

Homeopathic medicine is based on the principle that the more dilute the active ingredient in a remedy is, the more potent its effect. Does this sound counterintuitive to you? It does to me as well. A 12 C strength (on the centesimal scale, a single C is a hundred-fold dilution factor), a popular arnica strength for bruising, has been compared to adding a pinch of salt (an active ingredient) to the Atlantic Ocean. In fact, a 12 C strength only has a 60 percent chance of containing a single molecule of the original material. Still, homeopathic medicine is wildly popular and widely available. In addition, it appears to be safe—but only because the active ingredient is nearly absent.

I conducted my own research to see if arnica was of any benefit after eyelid surgery. Using a double-blind, placebo-controlled method (neither I the patients nor I knew if they were getting homeopathic arnica or an identical-appearing sugar pill), there was no difference in bruising or recovery. The results were highly statistically significant and published in a peer-reviewed journal.

I tell my patients that I believe homeopathic arnica is safe to take after cosmetic surgery, but I don't think there is any benefit either, based on direct scientific evidence. If your surgeon is recommending homeopathic arnica, he or she is either intentionally giving you a placebo or ignoring the lack of evidence to support homeopathy—or he or she is uninformed.

Bromelain (Pineapple Extract)

This concentrated form of pineapple enzymes has been described as having anti-inflammatory effects, including the reduction of prostaglandins that mediate inflammatory reactions in the body. It is also used as a meat tenderizer. Some research shows that it can help with wound healing when used on the surface of the skin, but little evidence shows that a pill form can help with surgical recovery. I'm not saying it doesn't work, but the studies aren't there yet. I have plenty of patients who eat an abundance of pineapples around the time of their surgery to minimize bruising. I can't promote this practice as being beneficial, but it shouldn't hurt.

Zinc

Zinc is an element that acts as a cofactor (a helper molecule) for many important processes that take place in our bodies at a molecular level, including some wound-healing activities. If you are deficient in zinc, then you need oral supplementation to prevent problems with recovery after a surgery or procedure. In people with normal levels of zinc, oral supplementation is less beneficial, but there is some evidence that topical zinc helps heal incisions and wounds by stimulating skin growth and preventing infection. There are zinc creams that promote wound healing, but these should be prescribed by your doctor.

CHAPTER 12

The Future of Cosmetic Treatments

The current state of cosmetic medicine provides hints about its future. Technological advances take place every year, and because there are major financial interests in cosmetic medicine, there will continue to be new options for those seeking rejuvenation.

Asia has been a major driving force for advances in aesthetics. There is a large (and growing) worldwide clamoring for minimally invasive procedures. I attended a conference in South Korea that was solely devoted to minimally invasive cosmetic procedures, and it was impressive to see the innovation and creativity born from consumer demand. In the late 1990s and early 2000s, we saw a dramatic shift to less-invasive technology led by the mainstream acceptance of injectable treatments (botulinum, collagen and hyaluronic fillers, and fat injections) and laser devices (fractional lasers and light-based treatments). The effectiveness and availability of nonsurgical and less-invasive surgical options are definitely on the rise.

Nanotechnology

Nanoparticles are extremely small, engineered materials. A nanometer is one-billionth of a meter, and nanoparticles are classified as materials that are less than one thousand nanometers—about the size of bacteria. In skin products, nanoparticle constituents can offer better penetration into the skin. This can mean that the product has the potential to be more effective or may have different properties than a product with larger particles. Topical skin products are currently the most commercially available use of nanotechnology.

Nanomachines are tiny, engineered materials that have active functions. In medicine, they may be used to mimic the action of natural cells (e.g., muscle, cartilage, etcetera), they may alter the composition of existing cells, or they may work as tiny robots, carrying out other tasks. These sound like the stuff of science fiction, but they actually exist, although they are not widely used or understood for medical applications—yet.

In cosmetic medicine, it is possible that a nanorobot could help replace cheek fat that was lost in the aging process by repairing or replicating fat cells. They could seek out skin that has sun damage and wrinkles and work to repair collagen and smooth out the ravaging signs of senescence. Obviously, a good deal of research and safety testing is in the way of actual implementation, but in a high-tech laboratory somewhere, someone is probably working on this right now.

Stem Cells

Also known as progenitor cells, stem cells have the potential to turn into any type of cell in the body. Think of them as cell babies. They are just waiting for the right set of circumstances to trigger them to develop and flourish. Stem cells are found in different parts of your body and are used to replenish existing cells that make up different tissues. They are found in bone marrow, blood (including blood in a newborn's umbilical cord), and fat tissue.

Stem cells can be directly injected under the skin with the aim of repairing and replenishing injured or depleted cells. It's still unclear how effective this approach is. When fat injections are performed in the face, we know that some stem cells are in the mix, but it's hard to separate which benefits come from the fat cells and which come from the surrounding soup that includes stem cells. It's also possible to culture stem cells and grow them in a laboratory after harvesting them from the body. These stem cells can be used in a similar way as the directly injected cells.

There are hopes that stem cells can revolutionize all of medicine by allowing doctors to treat a wide range of diseases and degenerative changes. As our understanding of this exciting facet of medicine grows, so should the practical applications for stem cells.

3-D Printers

Additive manufacturing, or 3-D printing, found its way into the mainstream vernacular in the early 2000s. It works in the same way that your computer printer transfers ink to make a 2-D image on paper—except the 3-D printer can use many different materials, and it can print three-dimensional objects. Some of these 3-D printers extrude melted materials one layer at a time while others use lasers or light to fuse powders into solid shapes. These printers are used to create custom commercial products, to fabricate prototype parts, and to sculpt artistic objects.

In medicine, 3-D printers have been used to print new skin, fabricate replacement jawbones, and grow the framework for new ears. Work is underway to print new organs. Imagine being able to construct a new body part to replace one that was damaged through injury or disease! What could athletes do with synthesized body parts to boost their sports performance? Cyborglike medical modifications are bathed in murky ethical waters that will challenge policy makers in the near future.

3-D printed skin and other organs can also be used to test new drugs, creams, and procedures. Your doctor will have the potential to practice your surgery or test a proposed therapy before applying it to your body.

3-D-printed custom chin implant next to a model of a patient's jaw

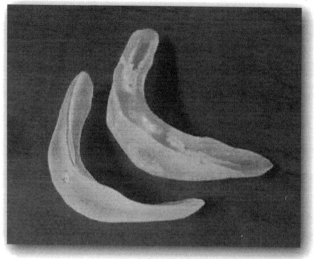

Lasers

Energy-based cosmetic solutions have generated the most buzz in the aesthetic marketplace for the last two decades. The word *laser*, when added to any procedure, makes it sound more modern, more precise, and more effective. *Laser facelift* sounds like a better version of a traditional facelift. Physicians use lasers to filter, focus, and intensify energy from light to affect some type of change in the body. Often, these changes are related to vaporization of tissue or controlled thermal tissue injury. Advances in laser medicine will allow doctors to have more control over this energy, more specifically target certain tissues, and deliver this energy with a higher degree of safety and efficacy.

Laser-assisted liposuction and lasers applied under the skin peaked in popularity around 2009, but they may see a resurgence if they can promise more skin tightening and cellulite improvement. Laser treatments for fat reduction and skin tightening are in high demand because they offer the possibility of rejuvenation and sculpting either without surgery or with minimal surgery.

Injections

Injectable cosmetic treatments largely consist of neurotoxins (Botox, Dysport, etcetera) and dermal fillers for facial wrinkle reduction and volume enhancement. New versions of these existing technologies will continue to be developed with enhanced features, such as more product longevity, higher safety profiles, and smoother, softer materials. Kelp-based fillers are currently being investigated and could potentially be less expensive to manufacture than the current hyaluronic-acid-based products. Dermal fillers are now being produced in larger-volume syringes based on the demand for higher-volume rejuvenation in areas such as cheeks, chin, and even breasts. Updated fillers can be placed closer to the surface of the skin without showing signs of discoloration or lumpiness while filling in shallow wrinkles that can be difficult to treat otherwise. Also being investigated is Botox in a cream form that for the first time may make possible a needleless Botox option.

Mesotherapy treatments are also poised to make a comeback. Mesotherapy is defined as the injection of a treatment agent into the mesoderm, or the tissues derived from the middle embryonic layers, which include the skin and the fat under the skin. Many different medicines and vitamins have been tested and tried as mesotherapy agents with the aim of treating many different conditions. When doctors perform mesotherapy, they are often using compounded agents that are mixed by a compounding pharmacist, and the treatment may not have been evaluated by the FDA. The most widespread treatments offered under the heading of mesotherapy target fat reduction and cellulite reduction using phosphatidylcholine, deoxycholate, and collagenase. One form of mesotherapy (ATX-101) was approved by the FDA for fat reduction under the chin, and this product will likely gain some popularity.

Platelet-rich plasma, or PRP, injections have been around for quite a few years now but have gradually picked up momentum as a legitimate treatment. PRP is a component of your own blood; it is extracted after a blood draw, and then it is isolated using a centrifuge. This part of the blood contains growth factors involved in your body's healing processes that take place on the molecular level. The idea is that these molecules signal your body to repair and regrow new tissues. PRP has been used in conjunction with surgery or laser treatments to help in wound healing and promote favorable scar formation, and it has been injected in a mesotherapylike way to rejuvenate the facial skin also. It's been termed the "vampire lift" because it comes from your own blood.

More Customization

Aesthetic treatments are highly personal. You are treating concerns and conditions that are specific to you: your anatomy and your genetics. The future of implants, injectable fillers, and facial contouring will use 3-D imaging to evaluate your specific shape and asymmetries. This precise evaluation will help to determine the size and shape of an implant or the placement and amount of filler injections needed to address your own desires based on sophisticated prediction models.

Genetic screening tests are already available that look at known genes that control how your body's cellular receptors respond to certain medications. These tests can predict how effective a pharmaceutical agent will be. For example, I underwent a genetic screening panel through a now-defunct company called Existence Genetics in California. It determined that a commonly used blood-thinning agent used to treat patients after heart attacks would be less effective for me than expected. If I develop heart disease in the future, I can provide this information to my physician so that my treatment regimen can be adjusted to my genetics. The same concept can apply to topical skin products. Genetic screening will be able to optimize a skin-care regimen that can be tailored to the receptors and chemistry in your skin. To envision a scenario further down the development pipeline, skin products with nanotechnology may have the ability to sense changes in your body's chemistry or in your surrounding environment and make relevant adjustments just as your smartphone can use your location and search history to adjust your phone's interface and your user experience.

Personal Health Dashboards

We have entered a phase of civilization where information, electronic or otherwise, is a commodity. There are more ways to obtain and record information than ever before. Some of the most relevant and compelling information in your personal data stream relates to you and your health. Digital pedometers started a trend in which we have access to tracking our daily activities, functions, and biological status. Health wristbands, smartphones, and other wearable devices currently have the ability to record, store, and report your heartrate, blood pressure, skin temperature, weight, body-fat percentage, sleep movements, calorie balance, ultraviolet exposure, and distance traveled, to name a few. As these monitors become more sophisticated, you will be able to monitor levels of blood components and other descriptive data points that can be transmitted to your doctor or graphically displayed on your smartphone. Some of this information will be used to prevent premature signs of aging.

CHAPTER 13

Beauty, Longevity, and Beauty Resources

Looking your best for the longest possible stretch of time requires attention and consistency. The steps in this book—beginning from the first signs of aging to skin strategies to individual facial areas—are all proven to work. You have to decide where you want to focus your resources and how you wish to prioritize. Start with the **pause** strategies at a minimum and then move on to the **reverse** strategies as you see fit (usually in the order of skin, and then eyes, and then neck).

Some of the same lifestyle choices that lead to overall longevity also promote beauty longevity. These include a healthy diet (low in processed foods, low in trans fats, and low in sugar), regular exercise, and avoidance of smoking.

Advice on Specific Lasers, Products, and Procedures

In the "Skin Maintenance and Repair" chapter, I recommended a basic regimen to halt skin aging and wrinkles, but I didn't give specific product names. There are many great product lines on the market (and many mediocre ones), and I don't want to favor or snub any one company. In addition, the product names change quite frequently. On my website, http://drkotlus.com/pause-andreverse, I list the products that I am currently recommending to some clients and that we are using in my household. This doesn't mean the products will be best for you (you may not like the fragrance or texture), but it is an endorsement of sorts; the product worked for me at a given point in time. You can also join in the discussion on the site and share which products you like and get advice from others.

This blog post on my website explains how to find out if a skin-care product is safe: http://www.drkotlus.com/find-skin-cream-safe.

On my blog, I regularly discuss procedures, lasers, and aesthetic devices that I think are effective and worthwhile: http://drkotlus.com/blog.

PubMed is a great resource for finding scientific medical articles on any topic. You can type in a supplement name, laser, or procedure and get an extensive list of studies and reviews that were published in peer-reviewed journals: http://www.ncbi.nlm.nih.gov/pubmed/.

RealSelf is a social-media-driven site containing reviews of surgeons and procedures and discussions about cosmetic surgery. Anything read here should be taken with a grain of salt as device companies and physicians have been known to game the system: http://www.realself.com.

Tools to Help You Stick to Your Plan

HabitForge is a web-based system that e-mails you on a daily basis to check in with you on specific goals you have set. It offers inspiration and asks if you've been attaining your goals. I tried it out with my sunscreen usage and I found it very helpful.

http://www.habitforge.com

Smartphone Apps

The Think Dirty app and the Skin Deep app help you find out if the ingredients in your skin products are safe by scanning the barcode on the side of the package.

http://www.thinkdirtyapp.com/

http://www.ewg.org/skindeep/app/

SkinBetter Skin Analyzer app allows you to take a photo of your skin with your phone's camera and it gives you an analysis of wrinkles, sun damage, and brown spots. If you start a new treatment plan, you can use this app to track your progress.

http://skinbetter.com/skinanalyzer/step1/index/

The Environmental Protection Agency (EPA) has a free app that gives you the ultraviolet index in your area by the hour.

http://developer.epa.gov/epa-uv-index/

Organizations and Doctor Directories

Many organizations have directories of cosmetic surgeons. In the United States, the American Board of Cosmetic Surgery has a list of certified cosmetic surgeons: http://www.americanboardcosmeticsurgery.org/.

Societies (not boards) that have directories include:

American Academy of Cosmetic Surgery; http://www.cosmeticsurgery.org

American Society of Aesthetic Plastic Surgery; http://www.surgery.org/consumers/find-a-plastic-surgeon

American Academy of Facial Plastic Surgery; http://www.aafprs.org/

American Society of Ophthalmic Plastic and Reconstructive Surgery; http://www.asoprs.org

At the time of this writing, many dermatologists perform cosmetic procedures, but there is no official directory for dermatologists who are aesthetically oriented. The American Academy of Dermatology has its own physician directory: https://www.aad.org/for-the-public.

To Your Health and Beauty

There has never been a better time to take advantage of everything the intersection of the beauty industry and medicine has to offer. I wish you success in achieving and maintaining your best, healthiest-looking self. When you go to your next class reunion, perhaps you'll be the youngest-looking one in the room!

39979901R00071

Made in the USA
Middletown, DE
31 January 2017